CAREER COMPASS
2nd Edition

Titles in the Series

The Bluejacket's Manual
Career Compass
Chief Petty Officer's Guide
Command at Sea
Developing the Naval Mind
Dictionary of Modern Strategy and Tactics
Dictionary of Naval Abbreviations
Dictionary of Naval Terms
Division Officer's Guide
Dutton's Nautical Navigation
Farwell's Rules of the Nautical Road
Fighting the Fleet
Fleet Tactics and Naval Operations
General Naval Tactics
International Law for Seagoing Officers
Naval Ceremonies, Customs, and Traditions
The Naval Institute Guide to Naval Writing
The Naval Officer's Guide
Naval Officer's Guide to the Pentagon
Naval Shiphandler's Guide
Newly Commissioned Naval Officer's Guide
Operations Officer's Guide
Petty Officer's Guide
Principles of Naval Engineering
Principles of Naval Weapon Systems
The Professional Naval Officer: A Course to Steer By
Reef Points
A Sailor's History of the U.S. Navy
Saltwater Leadership
Shiphandling Fundamentals for Littoral Combat Ships and the New Frigates
Surface Warfare Officer's Department Head Guide
Watch Officer's Guide

The U.S. Naval Institute
Blue & Gold Professional Library

For more than 100 years, U.S. Navy professionals have counted on specialized books published by the Naval Institute Press to prepare them for their responsibilities as they advance in their careers and to serve as ready references and refreshers when needed. From the days of coal-fired battleships to the era of unmanned aerial vehicles and laser weaponry, such perennials as *The Bluejacket's Manual* and the *Watch Officer's Guide* have guided generations of Sailors through the complex challenges of naval service. As these books are updated and new ones are added to the list, they will carry the distinctive mark of the Blue & Gold Professional Library series to remind and reassure their users that they have been prepared by naval professionals and meet the exacting standards that Sailors have long expected from the U.S. Naval Institute.

SECOND EDITION

CAREER COMPASS

Navigating the Navy's Officer
Promotion and Assignment System

DOUGLAS H. RAU

Naval Institute Press
Annapolis, Maryland

Naval Institute Press
291 Wood Road
Annapolis, MD 21402

© 2025 by the U.S. Naval Institute
All rights reserved. No part of this book may be reproduced or utilized in any form or by any means, electronic or mechanical, including photocopying and recording, or by any information storage and retrieval system, without permission in writing from the publisher.

Library of Congress Cataloging-in-Publication Data
Names: Rau, Douglas author
Title: Career compass : navigating the Navy's officer promotion and assignment system / Capt. Douglas Rau, USN (RET.), PHD.
Description: Second edition. | Annapolis, Maryland : Naval Institute Press, [2025] | Series: Blue & gold professional library | Revised edition of: Career compass : navigating through the Navy's officer assignment and promotion systems / James A. Winnefeld, Sr. 2005. | Includes bibliographical references and index.
Identifiers: LCCN 2025024160 (print) | LCCN 2025024161 (ebook) | ISBN 9781682476857 hardcover | ISBN 9781682479650 paperback | ISBN 9781682477717 ebook
Subjects: LCSH: United States. Navy—Promotions | United States. Navy—Officers' handbooks | LCGFT: Handbooks and manuals
Classification: LCC VB313 .W55 2025 (print) | LCC VB313 (ebook) | DDC 359.0023/73—dc23/eng/20250616
LC record available at https://lccn.loc.gov/2025024160
LC ebook record available at https://lccn.loc.gov/2025024161

♾ Print editions meet the requirements of ANSI/NISO z39.48-1992 (Permanence of Paper).
Printed in the United States of America.

9 8 7 6 5 4 3 2 1

CONTENTS

	Foreword	ix
	Preface *Starting at the Beginning: Planning Your Career*	xiii
	Acknowledgments	xvii
1	Performance: The Sine Qua Non	1
2	Your Boss Wants to See You Promoted but Needs Your Help	10
3	What Are They Saying About You?	22
4	What Should They NOT Be Saying About You?	28
5	Leveling the Playing Field	37
6	Spring Training	47
7	Do You Shine in the Career Marketplace?	58
8	Been to School Lately?	65
9	Sea/Shore Rotation and Homesteading	75
10	Command and Staff Assignments	81
11	Washington Duty	88
12	Career Tracks for the Unrestricted Line	98
13	Promotion to Flag Rank	108
14	Awards and Decorations	118

15	Pass the (Social) Polish, Please	124
16	The Navy Spouse and Family	132
17	Assignment and Placement Officers	139
18	The Fitness Report System	156
19	Screening and Promotion Boards: And the Verdict Is...	171
20	Advice for Midshipmen	177
21	Advice for Those Who Have Missed a Hurdle	184
22	Some Parting Shots	196
	Appendix A *Dilemmas and Paradoxes in a Naval Career*	209
	Appendix B *The Junior Officer's Professional Library*	219
	Notes	223
	Index	235

FOREWORD

I can imagine a no more rewarding career. And any man [or woman] who may be asked in this century what he [or she] did to make his [or her] life worthwhile, I think can respond with a good deal of pride and satisfaction: "I served in the United States Navy."

—President John F. Kennedy, August 1, 1963
Remarks at the United States Naval Academy
to the Plebe Class of 1967

The above words have inspired me since I entered Annapolis on June 30, 1964, with the class of 1968. When I was a young lieutenant in 1976, I had the privilege of working with the author of the first edition of *Career Compass*, Rear Adm. Jim Winnefeld, both as a company officer and as his executive assistant. He became a lifelong mentor and confidant. I have known no more capable and honorable naval officer in my career.

I have, for the past six years, taught one section of first-class midshipmen a leadership course anchored in Values and Principles. *Career Compass* is a text I use in this class to inspire a meaningful conversation about all aspects of managing one's career. While some of the material is dated, much of what Admiral Winnefeld penned twenty years ago remains relevant. It brilliantly captures the career requirements of what it means to go to sea and sail in harm's way.

This wonderful and timely revision of *Career Compass* is authored by another extraordinary naval officer I have known well for over fifty years, Capt./Dr. Doug Rau. He was a seasoned fleet 1200 psi engineer when I took the reins as chief engineer in USS *Fox* (CG 33) in 1978 and provided me the support and phenomenal performance to allow us to succeed in the most demanding tour of my career, save that of Chairman of the Joint Chiefs of Staff. There are those who would argue, I among them, that he saved my career.

Captain Rau's update to *Career Compass* is compelling. His rich experience in multiple communities (surface warfare officer/engineering duty officer), multiple ship types (frigates, cruisers, aircraft carriers), in command, and as the head community detailer provides a rare depth and breadth to every aspect of managing a naval officer's career from ensign to flag. His main message is: go to sea, take hard jobs, and above all, perform well. A naval officer should deploy often and carefully nurture one's reputation. He guides us through the fitness report system, the assignment system, and the "wickets" of promotion and screening boards along the way to command, which are the crucible through which great performance and successful careers are built.

I have read no better articulation of mentorship, which is part of Captain Rau's recipe of caring for those Sailors and their families whom we are charged to lead. He speaks of the growing requirement to "balance" one's life including the important focus on one's family, spousal careers, and financial stability. He rightly highlights getting to Washington (headquarters) early and often, as well as obtaining an advanced degree to enable growth and critical thinking. "If you are not growing, you are dying," one of my mentors advised.

Captain Rau's exceptionally robust update to a seemingly timeless original edition should be the guidebook for every naval officer.

Foreword

Its wisdom will help propel every reader to greater career success and a stronger Navy.

M. G. Mullen
Admiral, USN (Ret.)
28th Chief of Naval Operations
17th Chairman, Joint Chiefs of Staff

PREFACE

Starting at the Beginning
Planning Your Career

> I heard long ago in the Army: Plans are worthless, but planning is everything.
>
> —President Dwight D. Eisenhower[1]

Every Navy detailer brief outlines the timelines, requirements, qualifications, and expectations to complete a "successful" career in that Navy warfare area. The message from the community managers outlines the most likely path to travel in order to be promoted with your year group and to position you for a Navy command and promotion to the rank of captain. This book, *Career Compass*, is intended to support this ideal, with the purpose of pointing to and highlighting the principles that should keep every officer eligible and competitive for promotion and command while being competent and capable in performing the necessary duties supporting the requirements of the naval service.

Whether your aspirations include long-term service ending in a military retirement or the completion of your obligated service and a move into industry or government, the lesson from President Eisenhower should be considered. Having a plan to reach a personal goal is important to ensure you have the requisite experience and expertise to be competitive for positions leading to the goal. However, sticking strictly to an original plan amid constantly changing circumstances is probably not a good idea. Consider the triad of detailing: the needs of the Navy, promotion opportunities within your community, and your personal family goals. All are going to change over time. The *nominal* career path may not be what is right for you, and as presented in this text, you should regularly communicate with your family and the resources within your command, your warfare community, and the Navy Personnel Command to keep you on a path that is pointed to your true north.

When I entered the U.S. Naval Academy in 1970, I was expecting to be part of the Vietnam conflict—which ended just as we were graduating. The next decades were committed to operations supporting the Cold War, and I experienced a very different career and deployment cycle from what I had anticipated. Years later, specifically for those commissioned in the spring of 2001 or 2002, junior officers had no idea that the next two decades would require a heightened readiness to engage in the war on terrorism. The theater of interest, the rapid deployment cycles, and the extended times on station had not been part of their expectations. However, we must accept that there may always be "wars and rumors of wars,"[2] and the requirements for the Navy will necessarily adjust to meet the changing world conditions.

Career Compass is about planning—and replanning. It is about seeing opportunities and being prepared to successfully navigate the challenges ahead. Your service in the Navy is important to our nation and your family. You should have career and life goals in mind and an informed plan to achieve those goals. Hopefully, you will be aided in that quest with elements of this text.

In 2005 Rear Adm. James A. Winnefeld Sr. reflected on his lengthy Navy career, and particularly his extraordinary experience serving in the Bureau of Naval Personnel, in *Career Compass: Navigating Through the Navy's Officer Assignment and Promotion System*. A naval officer of any rank would benefit greatly by knowing the inside operations of the bureau and by considering the particular advice the admiral makes to be promoted in rank and selected for the ultimate goal of command.

In the twenty years since *Career Compass* was published, major elements of our world presence mission and core values have not changed. However, much has changed in our programs and management of the all-volunteer service. Repeals of the Don't Ask, Don't Tell policy (2010) and Combat Exclusion Act (2015) are notable. This second edition is intended to highlight some of the changes in culture, communication, routine, and career options for a Navy officer to navigate through a successful career of service. Sustained superior performance will remain the key to success, but the emphasis on mentoring, graduate education, sea-shore rotations, Washington duty, fitness reports, and tools to communicate with your community detailer should be noted. What is not included in this update are the all-important specifics on military pay and retirement. The incentive of pay and the projection of lengthy retirement benefits must be part of the individual (and family) consideration during the career path planning. Each fiscal year, the changes to military pay scales, along with the allowances and bonuses for eligible members, are made public. Additionally, retirement eligibility, benefits, and compensation are regularly changing as policymakers consider the necessary incentives to keep our volunteer service strong.

For more than twenty years I have had the honor to teach at the U.S. Naval Academy; interacting daily with the midshipmen and the (mostly) junior rotational officers has given me the opportunity to engage regularly in personal coaching and career mentoring. The tone of this second edition is meant to point the aspiring junior officers toward a successful Navy career. There is much to be gained in a career of service, and the opportunities ahead are going to be great!

ACKNOWLEDGMENTS

Just as one's career is accomplished through the direction, encouragement, and correction from many others, this updated edition of *Career Compass* was completed with much collective help. Most importantly, Adm. Michael G. Mullen, USN (Ret.), asked me to assist in teaching his leadership course to 1/C midshipmen at the U.S. Naval Academy and encouraged me to update this book as a helpful guide for the graduating midshipmen. Reviews of process and program changes and amplification of career expectations were added by the various community managers and detailers at the Navy Personnel Command and by the collection of post–major command Navy officers who now serve at the academy. These experienced and helpful reviewers are not responsible for errors and opinions that are expressed in the text.

I owe deep gratitude to Mr. Steve Catalano, senior acquisitions editor of the Naval Institute Press, for his patience and helpful direction as I navigated the course in my first publication with the press. My additional thanks to Ms. Jessica Sparks, editorial assistant, for her help in gathering the collection of photographs that help to illuminate the messages that are intended in the text. A special personal appreciation goes to Capt. Tasya Lacy, USN, for her regular review and encouragement to personalize this career planning guide.

Finally, as outlined in this text, coaches and mentors should be regular assets to help direct the course of one's career. Rear Adm. George R. Yount, USN (Ret.), was my example of a Navy officer who took the hard jobs and sustained the highest level of performance. He was my mentor and more of a champion as he guided me in my career decisions and kept our personal and professional friendship strong throughout our careers and into retirement.

—Capt. Douglas H. Rau, PhD, USN (Ret.)

1

PERFORMANCE
The Sine Qua Non

> The quality of your naval career, whether short or long, is solely dependent on your performance. Whether you get the plum assignments and whether or not you get promoted is based solely and wholly on your performance.
> —Vice Adm. Robert F. Dunn, USN (Ret.)

When using the original *Career Compass* text as a required reading in a leadership course during my years of teaching at the Naval Academy, midshipmen have reported that the message of this book is simple: take hard jobs, and perform well. While you don't always have control over the first part, it is up to you how you perform in the assigned positions you do have. The simple truth is that the hard jobs and subsequent promotions are granted for sustained superior past performance, the potential for future superior performance, and the needs of the service for your demonstrated skills. There is no shortcut or fast track. One of the glories of the naval service is that success and significance come down to you—what you put into the quest and your acquired inventory of professional skills.

A caution in this early section is that one might see superior performance as necessary and solely a transactional effort. Work hard, perform well, and you will be rewarded with promotions and more hard (good) jobs. While that is generally true, the negative consequences of poor performance are also certainly true. But one should consider that performance is more of an obligation than an option. In our oath of office, there is a clear commitment to "well and faithfully discharge the duties of the office upon which I am about to enter."[1] There are no qualifiers here for the position title, type of work, level of difficulty, or expectations of additional reward or recognition. The oath we take should remind us that we are committed to doing all that is necessary to fulfill the expectations of the specific, current assignment we have and the general obligations of being a leader of character in the U.S. Navy.

In the officer qualification pipeline, it behooves one to make the concerted effort to work and study hard to complete the required training and to score well on exams, but more importantly to understand the skills and principles of one's chosen career field and to be best prepared for the following leadership assignments on a ship, submarine, or squadron. Outlined in Chief of Naval Operations Instruction 3120.32,[2] the "Standard Organization and Regulations of the U.S. Navy" (SORM), the Chief of Naval Operations (CNO) outlines the expectations for the officers assigned to any position of authority in a Navy command. Tailored for each command, the ship's SORM provides the overarching and specific basic functions, duties, responsibilities, and authorities, and the organizational relationship for the command's positions with the expectation that these will be assigned and executed with professional excellence.

Performance assessment, however, is more than just what you do; it includes the evaluation of how well you do it. In the way you complete your assignment, are you contributing to the overall mission, advancing the abilities of the command, creating a positive environment that supports and encourages your seniors and subordinates alike? The type of performance questions to be considered include: Are you competent, compassionate, and courageous?[3] Are you attentive, firm, and fair? Are you well liked, and do you present a positive reflection on your command and the Navy? Mostly subjective in nature, these questions lead to a simpler assessment: can you be trusted—in things big and small? The Navy Performance Evaluation System[4] provides the feedback in the form of the officer fitness report (FITREP) for you to be evaluated in overall performance that includes the assessment of tactical proficiency, leadership, and personal engagement in fostering a command and workplace environment conducive to the growth and development of all personnel.

Creating the environment for your personal growth, development, and advancement is certainly primary in the career equation. As you plan your future and receive regular evaluations of your performance, there will be opportunities to learn, grow, and demonstrate your personal value and contributions to your command and your potential for more challenging assignments in the future.

Sustained Superior Performance as the Independent Variable

Superior performance in your current job is the entering argument in qualifying for promotion. Even better is sustained superior performance in a tough job under tough conditions. Best of all is a combination of the above with the results being recorded by an able writer of FITREPs. Note how performance enters into each step of this process:

1. qualifying for a demanding job in the first place (based on past performance)

2. performing well in a tough job
3. performing while forward deployed, in combat, or both, and
4. serving under a skipper[5] who can document performance in a way that is convincing to a selection or screening board.

Although luck plays some role in each step of the process, ambitious officers exert themselves at each step, whether lucky or not. For example, qualifying for a demanding job means seeking logical precursor assignments, working on the deck plates to become a professional, and looking for and not avoiding the tough jobs. Some jobs have the reputation for being arduous and sometimes apparently thankless. Why not prepare for or pick the one that has the least risk or work associated with it? Why not pick the one where the challenges are those with which one is most comfortable? Don't do it! You will only set yourself up for disappointment. Those who perform the toughest jobs under the most demanding conditions are the career winners.

The last step in good performance, as noted, is a commanding officer (CO) who can document performance in the one official document that must be reviewed at selection boards—the officer fitness report. What appears to be a thankless position may be the result of the command's inability to officially record the importance of the role and the effort and success of assigned officer. FITREPS are a vital part of your professional curriculum vitae or résumé; the topic will be woven into many sections and in many ways in this text.

Keep in mind that even when it comes to writing your fitness report, you are not without influence. COs want, and are directed, to obtain your input before the first draft report is written. They want you to tell them about your accomplishments and your desires as to future assignments. The key is to give your busy executive

Performance

officer (XO) and CO phrases, sentences, and even paragraphs that can be inserted with little change into your fitness report. If asked, provide a draft FITREP that is good enough so the only changes required might be in the style preferred by your boss. Therefore, document your accomplishments throughout the reporting cycle to make this process easier for you. It is much harder to recall a year's worth of work in a short time frame. Additionally, be diligent about receiving and responding to midterm counseling. This submission is not a sneaky or underhanded endeavor. COs and XOs are busy people, as you will find out, and the easier you make their jobs, the more your true value is appreciated and documented. They are human; they cannot remember everything. It is up to you to help them tactfully and without fanfare. A side benefit of this preparation is that you will learn to write reports of fitness before you get in the skipper's chair.

Still, you may encounter at least one difficult assignment environment where you will prepare yourself, work hard, and do all the right things—and not get all the credit you believe you deserve. Ship's schedules change, significant technical issues hold ships in port or aircraft on the ground, and there are scheduled maintenance and overhaul periods that may limit your opportunity to engage in your "primary" warfighter role. Although the best people are picked for the precommissioning crew, such assignments are not under the same spotlight as overseas deployments. These are the times to be creative and helpful for yourself and your subordinates to further operational experience and learn more of the intricacies of their ship or aircraft. This may be the time to do cross-rate training, cross-deck underway periods, and engagement with the maintenance community to facilitate repairs and testing. Those ashore or in the restricted-line communities can expect tours with similar challenges. The shore assignments may be more demanding than your "shore-duty" expectation. Gaps in billets, special staff projects, and rotations on the watch floor can be especially demanding on your work-life balance. The bottom line is that when confronting the difficult assignment, be professionally engaged and look for any opportunity to be an active participant in the completion of these necessary events to get back to sea or flight or some normalcy in work routine.

Naval officers may not be noted for their introspection. But all, either knowingly or not, keep themselves and their tasks in perspective. They do want to be promoted, but first and foremost, they want to do a tough job well and later seek the regard of fellow officers and the crew. Focusing on and following the old nautical adage of priorities—"ship, shipmate, self"—is still good advice. The most dangerous naval officers are those who reverse these priorities and want to be promoted at any price. When they game the system, they do it to achieve personal advantage. These officers see life as a zero-sum game, gloat about the professional misfortunes of others, are loath to share the credit for a job well done, look at every challenge with an eye to what is in it for them, and look for their next job before they really settle into their current one. They are not officers; they are careerists. And the demands of the profession uncover them sooner or later. Striking a balance between ambition and service is among the most crucial judgments officers make as they proceed through a naval career.

Needs of the Navy

The handmaiden of good professional performance, and one side of the detailer's triad, is the oft-misused phrase "needs of the Navy."[6] What does it mean? In short, it labels billets that need to be filled, the priority accorded to filling them, and the quality of the officer needed to fill them. "Quality" means the qualifications of the officer needed (experience, education, and demonstrated ability). Quality always involves a performance dimension as well as the credentials dimension. For example, some billets call for a post-command commander who, at a minimum, had an earlier command tour that was marked as successful. The phrase "needs of the Navy" is often part of the argument used to justify assigning an officer to a billet they do not desire. It could be a good billet—command—and the officer assigned has just come from a successful command tour. Sometimes an officer who had just returned home from a command tour in a deployed unit was "ripped out" and sent to another similar command (perhaps deployed) where the previous skipper had been hospitalized or relieved for other reasons. The needs of the Navy dictated a quick transfer at considerable personal cost to the officer.

But more often, the needs of the Navy send you to an assignment that is difficult to fill for another reason. No one wants it, or it has been left vacant ("gapped") too long. Your negotiating power is limited in these circumstances, but you might either negotiate with the detailer to short-tour you in such a job or perform so well that you warrant special treatment for a follow-on assignment. To find yourself in such an unwanted job will try your soul. It has happened at least once in many careers, and the only way the officer could overcome the handicap was to redouble efforts to achieve top performance—to the point where the detailer could not afford to leave the officer there. Detailers have a demand for more top-quality officers than exist. So they must marshal this quality resource carefully. One cannot afford to put top officers into less demanding or low-leverage jobs.

But there is another dimension to "needs of the Navy." Some subspecialties will be in more demand today than they were yesterday. Some trends can be predicted, and others cannot. You should attempt to acquire professional tools that will be most needed in the Navy of the future. The selection board precepts identify these special needs and direct the boards to give special consideration to the current and prospective issues. Every so often, officers will be promoted, even to high rank, not because they were at the top in the performance dimension but because they had a specialty that was critically needed at their selected rank. So although performance is the most important horse in the race, credentials can become a critical factor in some cases.

Although it is a truism to state that we carry the seeds of future promotions in our performance to date, this obvious fact is often obscured by our obsession with the politics of the game—and luck, both good and bad. There is simply no easy path to command and promotions. You must get the selection board's trust the old-fashioned way: you must earn it. It is not a matter of touching all the bases in a good career progression. It is not the warfare pins you wear, the decorations on your chest, or the people you know; it is how you do the job that counts. It helps if the job is tough, the environment is tougher, and your skipper is toughest. But it starts and ends with you.

There are two vignettes appropriate for consideration of your performance. First is a lesson in leadership development. The question was posed to a senior officer: what must I do to best prepare myself for future assignments? The answer: "Identify those elements of your current job or assignment that you like doing the least . . . and concentrate on making those elements what you do the very best."[7] Success will require you to do well in all aspects of your assignment, especially in what you don't like doing at all.

Second is a detailer's response. Junior officers in my community repeatedly asked questions concerning the best jobs, the best locations, the best bosses to pursue in order to be most competitive for promotions. As the senior detailer, I wish I had the answer offered by the actor/comedian Steve Martin in a 2007 interview. "Nobody ever takes note of [my advice], because it's not the answer they wanted to hear," Martin said. "What they want to hear is 'Here's how you get an agent, here's how you write a script,' . . . but I always say, 'Be so good they can't ignore you.'"

Are you the person who will always be an active supporter of the team's success? Hold yourself and others accountable? Learn from mistakes? Continue to learn from experience? Help others succeed? Do you see personal sustained superior performance as an obligation and not an option? Are you so good you cannot be ignored?

2

YOUR BOSS WANTS TO SEE YOU PROMOTED BUT NEEDS YOUR HELP

> Our country! In her intercourse with foreign nations may she always be in the right; but our country, right or wrong.
> —Commo. Stephen Decatur

The Golden Anchor Award (now the Retention Excellence Award) is the annual recognition for sustained superior levels of military retention within ships, squadrons, staffs, and shore commands.[1] The gold-painted anchor is a visible recognition of a command that promotes a culture of excellence and supports the need for attracting and retaining the best talent within our Navy forces. While the presentation of the award centers on the commanding officer, the command master chief, and the command career counselor, the reality is that every member of the command contributes to the positive assessment. Your success is reflected in the success of the command, and the success of the command is likewise attributed to your contribution. You are, or become, one of that command's "team."

All skippers glory in a high retention rate and a high promotion rate in their command. A little-recognized fact is that your boss benefits when you *ship over* or are promoted. The Golden Anchor, after all, is a testimonial to their leadership in creating the culture and environment that encourages and enables a long-term commitment to the Navy. Most commanders will be bashful about it, but they attribute your advancement and promotion to their training, nurturing, and correction when needed. No CO ever took joy in a low shipping-over rate. The point is that you have a built-in advantage as you strive to perform well in your current billet: your CO wants you to succeed, and most will work hard to see that you do. But your CO cannot do it alone.

Be skeptical when you hear the comment, "My skipper had it in for me." When you pull the string on that comment, you often hear such self-serving excuses as, "Well, I didn't kowtow to him," "I told her like it was," "I stood up for my people," "I didn't make him look good," "I didn't kiss-up to her," and so on. You get the idea. Behind each excuse lies the real reason, which is less flattering to the speaker. Your CO deserves your study, not your excuses. You study your bosses not only because your future success is in their hands, but also because you just might learn from them. COs are human, but they also have a job to do. That job is rarely easy, and they must do it through the efforts of you and your shipmates. If they cannot do that, they fail.[2]

As you mature in the service, you come to realize that the real heavy lifting of the Navy's work gets done not through giving peremptory orders (though some are needed) but through guiding and motivating subordinates. If you seem to be getting an inordinate amount of undesired, and in your perception undeserved, attention from your CO, it is probably the result of their judgment that you need prodding, guidance, or butt-kicking to get the command's and your jobs done. You can fight your COs on this, or you can learn from them. The former may make you feel better and more self-righteous (momentarily), but the latter is the more constructive course. Everyone has had some bosses one did not like, but there is not a single one from whom the subordinate could not learn and become a better officer for it. The point of all this: make your CO your ally in the performance and promotion business, not your adversary. How is this done? Let us look at a few paths you might explore.

Who Is the "Go-To" Officer in Your Outfit?

Every command has a small number of junior officers who are so versatile, so willing to do the toughest jobs, so full of gusto and a sense of adventure, that they become in effect the "911" staff for the command. Special or priority projects migrate to them—not because they need to be dumped on but because they are so able, willing, and can-do. They are the treasures of the command, the first people the CO, XO, or department heads turn to when they need something important done in a hurry and done well. Most often the task falls outside the younger officer's narrow billet description. No matter, though. They get on with it, and a miracle occurs: they get their shipmates to help them or smooth the path for them. The applicable adage I learned on my first command was that if you want something done, give it to a busy person. There were those few who, regardless of the tasking, always seemed to be organized, positive, and productive. Rather than debate or deflect, they just got the job done.

You may follow the old salt's advice and never volunteer and never offer unsolicited information, but you can also never try to get out of an onerous task. Your reputation will spread like wildfire where it counts. It is not that you are a pushover; it is that you are the only person to get the really tough and often dirty jobs. A reputation as the "go-to" and "can-do" officer is twenty-four-carat gold at fitness report time, and the attribute will leave a mark in the minds of the command and the selection board members.

Who Is the Most Positive Officer in Your Outfit?

Every command has its share of gloomy Gusses, skeptics, and sour apples. They never met an order or a boss they liked. Their last command was dramatically better than the current. They are the first to see the difficulties, shortcomings, loopholes, and downside of any order or task they are given. They may state, and restate, the days left until their end of obligated service, and their long-term objective is simply to get to their active duty release date or rotation date. Their short-term objective seems to be to make life as depressing as possible for their shipmates. As a result, they are hard to get moving, and they question the need for the task and the way it is to be done. They are never morale boosters, and their best company is like-minded souls.

On the other hand, there are the enthusiasts, the "red hots," the "let's get it done yesterday" types who are the outfit's hard chargers. They occasionally overrun or miss the mark but never have to be prodded. It is their boss's job to provide fire control, not firepower. Although no wardroom or ready room needs many of these people, they really stand out and are the joy of most skippers. Those skippers will forgive them a lot so long as they are responsible and willing to be instructed. Enthusiasm is catching. It may not be stylish to some, but it is a force multiplier and guaranteed to get your boss's attention, and you will soon find the tough and good jobs coming your way.

If you are looking for one example or opportunity to exercise this enthusiasm, be an integral part of the ship's/sub's in-port damage control response team. The after-hours and weekend routine of damage control drills can be tedious and demoralizing if not led by an energized and enthusiastic cross-divisional leadership team. Every Marine is a rifleman, and every Sailor is a damage control-man. Regardless of your primary assignment, be the spark plug that can fire up any duty section to understand the purpose and importance of damage control training. The ultimate goal is for every crew member to be qualified and confident in their role to protect the ship/sub.[3]

Do You Have the Solution to the Problem?

For some people, it is sufficient to frame the problem (and it is important to consider the fundamental issues creating a problem). However, therein lies the distinction between analysts and executives. Executives must not only correctly formulate the problem but also solve it. Never, ever take a problem to the boss without (at least in your own mind) also developing a range of solutions. And you may not have a lot of time to do so. You cannot take the time to do a study of the options and the costs and benefits. You must be ready now, and this takes some mental preparation before the problem is encountered.

Consider what you hear or perceive the command's problems to be and practice in your mind what the various solutions might be and what you would do about them if you were in command. This is mentally "fleeting up." It should be part of your daily training. Start thinking in terms of "if I were in the skipper's shoes." This training can start at the ensign level and be refined as you get more experience.

Before getting too far over your skis, however, the more you know of the specific technical and personal issues within your division, squadron, or department, the better you will respond to questions about training plans, system casualties, and operational alternatives. As an officer with systems oversight, you will be expected to provide expert advice to your commander. If you are uncertain or unable to answer the most specific questions, be sure to bring along your chief or your most capable and experienced Sailor.

In addition to this mental preparation, seize every opportunity to train yourself to think on your feet. When a question is posed to someone else, put yourself through the mental gymnastics of formulating your own answer. Mental agility and a nose for the fundamentals in any situation will serve you well at every step in your career. Most times, the good, fast solution is better than the better, tardy one. Too many officers want to have it all right, all the time, but that can't be, and getting to that 100 percent point will hold you back. You should be ready to make a recommendation based on the "80 percent solution." As Gen. George Patton recognized, "A good plan violently executed now is better than a perfect plan executed next week."[4]

As a junior officer with four years' experience as a cruiser main propulsion assistant, I worked for three different department heads. Each brought differing experiences and expectations to the engineering department, yet they each relied heavily on my ability to assess plant and personnel performance and to make sound recommendations, and they regularly accepted my opinions and input. A bit of advice I received early was to be "quick to listen, and slow to speak." While I greatly appreciated the confidence shone my way, before speaking up (too fast), I needed to carefully consider the basis and implications of my advice and to acknowledge any limitations on my own understanding.

When You Are the Briefer, Do You Know the Subject Better than Anyone Else?

Briefings are one of the keys to your future. Whether it is a briefing to your Sailors, fellow officers in the wardroom or ready room, or the CNO, your service reputation either is being built or rests on the outcome. This book is not a primer on public speaking or "briefmanship," but it should highlight the importance of this skill in supporting your professional reputation. Suffice to say that you should get all the practice you can and prepare yourself meticulously for every presentation. Every reasonable question must be anticipated and an answer prepared. Briefers must mentally sit in the chairs of the audience and judge whether they have achieved clarity, completeness, and purpose. Does the briefing lead to a conclusion and a recommendation, or does it lead to another briefing?

Your primary objective in preparing for a briefing is simple: you must know more about the subject than anybody else in the room. You are assumed by your audience to be the expert. If you are not, someone else should be giving the briefing. Your second objective must be to package the information in a form the audience can understand and remember. Reflect on the ultimate importance of a preflight or underway brief. Lives are at stake, and the dissemination of critical directions must be clear to all members of the team.

A briefing is a test of your ability to organize your thoughts, present material in a logical manner, and communicate visually and orally. It is also a test of your ability to think on your feet, deal with the unexpected, and exercise tact while conveying information. Careers have been made on superlative briefing skills and in-depth knowledge of the subject being briefed. The Navy's Fighter Weapons School (Top Gun) recognizes the importance of these skills and places extraordinary emphasis on them in qualifying both instructors and students. Repetitive "murder boards," which are group critiques of briefing content, format, and delivery, put each neophyte instructor and student-briefer through the wringer.[5] It is time well spent, and students and members of the staff gain a skill that will serve them well throughout their lives.

A regular concern, or maybe excuse, is that "I am not good, and don't like public speaking." Okay, so get over that!

Is There a Writer in the House?

Whereas good warfare specialty performance is the bedrock of a naval officer's professional competence, good writing skills are arguably second. Many officers have good warfare specialty skills; alas, few have good writing skills. At some point you will observe that the good job or the career-enhancing task seeks out the good writer. In any ship or squadron (or office), usually only a few officers are also good writers—that is, those who can use good English with a powerful effect. Clarity, brevity, and directness are the prized characteristics.

Acquiring this skill takes hard work and practice. Put your best effort into anything written that goes up the chain of command. An excellent place to practice is in writing the performance evaluations for your enlisted men and women. This practice will carry over later in your career in writing reports of fitness on your officers. See a problem? Put it in writing. Such writing not only polishes your drafting skills but also teaches the fundamentals of clear thinking. Official reports are the stage on which your command's performance is viewed. Early on you may have the arduous assignment to conduct a command investigation; while the assistance of a Navy JAG (judge advocate general) may be required to help with the technical requirements of the report, the overall value of the final report may rest in your ability to clearly and effectively communicate the root causes, recommendations, and critical applications of lessons to be learned. If you can write the tough or delicate paper, report, or letter for the CO, you will be considered a treasure.

On a more routine and mundane level, be aware that daily communications in emails and logbooks reflect your professionalism and attention to details. A quote attributed to numerous authors is, "If I had more time, I would have written a shorter letter."[6] The message from me (and for me) is to make the time to review, proofread, and be concise and direct in the messages that you wish to convey via electronic media. Before you hit send, be sure you consider how the message will be received (and retained).

Is there a "surrogate" writer in the house? In recent years, generative artificial intelligence has become a technology that is exciting, enabling, and at the same time disconcerting to the academic, professional, and technical communities. With remarkable ability to quickly create programs and text, this technology is being readily used for research papers, coding, and résumés. The eventual impact on standard military reports is yet to be realized, but it is a technology to watch as a helpful tool to augment good writing skills.

Are You a Pro?

Your most important skill is professional competence. In a previous charge of command, CNO Admiral Richardson outlined authority, responsibility, accountability, and expertise as the essential principles at the heart of command.[7] And it is the competence and character that lead to trust and the confidence to delegate and lead. Do you "know your stuff"? Do you skate to get by, or are you the person your chief petty officer or department head knows has the right answers or knows where to get them? Professional competence is so fundamental that it overrides such faults as a colorless or abrasive personality, poor writing style, poor manners, a sloppy uniform, or lack of initiative. I am not suggesting these failings are trivial—only that if you are professionally competent, you are worth the effort expended to shape you up. This means that if you are the main propulsion assistant, you know more about the engineering plant than any officer in the ship—including your boss, whose span of control is much larger. If your boss is more informed about your job than you are—and you do not change that relationship over time—that individual is doing your job for you. You know your plant and your division better than the boss does—or else.

To be called a competent pro by your shipmates and squadron mates is the ultimate accolade. It is the one you must strive hardest to achieve. It lies completely within your power to achieve it. Your boss will be one of the first to sense your achievement and applaud it.

If there is a single most important building block to a successful career, becoming a competent professional is it. It is your primary objective from the first time you report aboard. And from your first assignment, the Sailors working for you know you are not a pro, and are not competent or qualified for the ultimate positions that you will hold. What the Sailors do expect, however, is that you will continue to apply and assert yourself to be competent and qualified as quickly as possible. Consider that base questions posed in the *Officer Professional Core Competencies Manual*: Do you know the facts as they relate to your job? Can you interpret these concepts and principles as you see new situations? Can you apply your understanding of facts ideas to these situations? Can you demonstrate the ability to complete the tasks?[8]

In-port officer of the deck (OOD) may seem mundane, but it is your first step in joining the command's watch team and moving toward the more arduous underway/flight qualification. Be the best, most alert, and attentive OOD right off the bat. In all Navy communities, there is a progression of steps toward warfare qualification and command. In the job that you have right now, in the first watch qualification assigned—strive to do it very well.

Do You Help Your Command Solve People Problems?

Most of the problems and challenges faced by a ship or squadron involve people. Every officer in the command has a role in seeing that subordinates are led well, with sensitivity, and with an eye to making each member of the unit a contributor to the command's mission. That role does not change as you rise in rank and take on more responsible positions; your central focus remains the mission and the subordinates you are trying to motivate, direct, and care for.

Unfortunately, some officers create more personnel problems than they solve. Sometimes this is a matter of inexperience; in other cases, it is a matter of personal style in interactions, and in still others, it is a matter of interpersonal misunderstandings. On the other hand, some officers seem to be personnel problem solvers. They know their subordinates, they maintain open communications up and down, and they deftly use the resources at their disposal. They know what problems they can help solve, and they know when they need the help of their seniors.

This book is not about "deck plate leadership"; it is about professional performance that leads to command and promotions. Yet interpersonal skills are a critical element in that performance mix. Look closely at your shipmates who lead enlisted personnel well. In most cases you will find that they are good listeners, they empathize with their subordinates' problems, they do not take themselves too seriously, and they are firm in insisting on high standards for themselves and those who work for them. When you have to appear with one of your subordinates at captain's mast, you should ask yourself how you and the errant Sailor got there and what you might have done differently. Likewise, when you see the promotion lists, you should ask yourself why more of your people were not on it.

Perhaps the best reputation you can gain within your command is one of fostering respect up and down the chain of command. The first rule in George Washington's list of *Rules of Civility and Decent Behaviors in Company and Conversation* is: "Every Action done in Company, ought to be with Some Sign of Respect, to those that are Present."⁹ Be the officer who knows his or her Sailors, and be the officer who instinctively understands the reaction on the mess decks to a change in policy or circumstance. Treat all with dignity and respect, and you will be a better department head, executive officer, and skipper if you understand your Sailors on the basis of having had daily and close contact with them.

Inevitably, these identified skills will help you to be the better contributor to the command's mission and will get the recognition of your leadership and therefore find their way into your fitness reports and thence to the promotion selection boards. Your success and that of your command are mutually inclusive!

Before closing out a chapter relating to your reputation and your relationship with your boss, I wish to reflect on the chapter's epigraph and a lesson in leadership. Your boss may be hard to understand or hard to get along with. Your CO or XO may not be doing all they could to promote your career, and where does that leave you? As a junior officer, in a conversation with my commanding officer, I flippantly (and incorrectly) recited Decatur's quote by saying, "My Captain, may you ever be right, but right or wrong, my Captain!" After a long pause and a stern look, my captain asked, "Where did you get that idea?" After making me recite my oath of office, he reminded me that my commitment was to the Constitution, not a person, AND if he (my captain) was wrong, I had better have the courage to speak up, point that out, and make the correction.[10] Not every commanding officer will be easy or fun to work for. Despite the commander's personality, you and your subordinates need you to be professional, tactful, and competent to lead well. So, lead well!

3

WHAT ARE THEY SAYING ABOUT YOU?

> Leadership is like beauty because it's hard to define, but you know it when you see it.
>
> —Warren Bennis, leadership expert

It is a small world. The Navy is not as big as you may think. Your reputation is making the rounds—and has been for years. It is built like a house, brick by brick, good tour by good tour. You have a vested interest in seeing that your reputation is a good one. The previous chapter highlighted some of the more recognized competencies helpful to your (and your commander's) professional reputation. However, your reputation is defined by more than just a solid or subpar professional performance. Are you a good shipmate? Do you take care of your people? Are you overly concerned with your own promotion or assignments? How do you handle stressful situations or bad news? Is your family a positive reflection of your career? Do you party hard? Are you a good friend and colleague? The composite of all these factors defines your reputation. It is passed by word of mouth at any gathering of officers or their spouses. You will hear questions like the following: "Since you just came from USS *Neversail*, you must know Lieutenant So-and-so." "While you were going through Top Gun, was Lieutenant X on the staff?" "Was Commander Sea still there when you were at the War College?" And on it goes. Although some of this is gossip, most of it is an attempt to catch up on news of friends and to establish links among people in conversation.

John Masters, a career army officer and later a successful novelist, wrote a memoir of his growing up as a junior officer in the Indian army of the 1930s. He had many bumps in his army career, particularly as he learned the hard lessons of being a good messmate and a dependable officer. One of his observations goes directly to the importance of a service reputation and its relationship to performance: "The regiment did nothing overt to improve my character; it left that to me, giving me only good and bad examples and leaving me to draw my own conclusions. And I saw that ability was not really very important. It was for the conscientious, thoughtful, brave, and above all, straightforward man that people gave their best."[1]

One does not have to accept Masters' assessment of the lesser importance of professional ability to benefit from his penetrating insight as to how character affects reputation. Think of professional reputation as a matrix. On one dimension are people who know you: officers who are retired, active duty seniors, contemporaries, and juniors. The other dimension is time: when you were a midshipman or at officer candidate school (OCS), a junior officer, a senior officer, and today at whatever rank you hold. Each of the cells in this matrix contains people whose reflection on and opinion of you, taken together, define your service reputation. You might do well in one cell or in one time period and not so well in others. None should be overlooked as you conduct a self-assessment.

It is particularly easy to overlook two groups in your personal reflection, juniors and retired officers, but you do so at your professional peril. As for retired officers, bear in mind that some of them were probably your CO's boss at one time. In other cases, they may remember your performance more clearly than some active duty officers. Additionally, many retirees remain well plugged in to current Navy decision-making at all levels. Senior officers sometimes ask retired officers for advice; thus, to have your name mentioned favorably by a retired officer to an active duty officer can do a great deal of good: "I knew him when he was my chief engineer on USS *Eversail*."

As for juniors (to include enlisted Sailors), they may easily end up on a staff or future command to which you are subordinate. Their conversation in the staff meetings might bring reflections and opinions of your past engagements. The Sailors, whether they reenlist or leave the Navy, have a huge impact on future Navy recruiting and retention. You can control the narrative through your continuous positive and professional interaction with all whom you encounter.

Do not underestimate the lasting impact (positive or negative) that you have on your subordinates. To emphasize this point, I wish to reflect on a very recent personal story. In the time frame of editing *Career Compass*, I was surprised to receive an unsolicited note from Steven Lema, a Sailor who was in my engineering division aboard the USS *Fox* (CG 33) forty-eight years ago. His note clearly reflects the intended message here:

> Throughout my twenty years active, then into the reserves, I have maintained some and keep in contact with *Fox* Sailors. No matter, if I met a former *Fox* member at another command, household, or some other environment, never was there a time when we didn't talk about the *Fox* and the members that we served along with. In every conversation . . . every individual/servicemember of the *Fox* always had kind compliments of you [Ensign Rau]. I believe officers like yourself have passed on valuable characteristics that made a difference not only in our careers, but also in our own personal life.

Next to juniors and retired officers, the most overlooked cells of service reputation are those of contemporaries. I have come to the view over many years that it is your reputation among your contemporaries that is decisive. Seniors, more often than we like, can size you up incorrectly, but in my experience your contemporaries almost never do so. Good advice to senior officers in selecting a junior officer for assignment to their staff is to poll not just seniors for whom the candidate has worked but also the candidate's contemporaries. They will know how solid the officer is, how balanced are they in their social life and career, how well they can handle uncertain situations, and how can they be trusted in the large and small things.

The point of this discussion is that you cannot just rely on a one-dimensional perspective of service reputation. You must look across the board and across time. It is not enough to wish for your seniors to become successful and influential mentors; your contemporaries and juniors should be similarly blessed by your positive helpful example.

I am not suggesting here that you must butter up juniors and contemporaries—or seniors, for that matter. Rather, you must treat people as shipmates and colleagues, not stepping stones. Later, after you have retired, some of your more touching experiences will include being approached by an old shipmate and thanked for helping when in need or providing the necessary motivation through a chewing out or a hammering at a disciplinary hearing years earlier. There is no greater compliment than to just hear, "Thank you, I needed that." Mental toughness and honesty will guide you through those shoals. You are living dangerously if you dismiss the good honest opinions of juniors, contemporaries, and retired officers as unnecessary to your future success.

To sum up: Your FITREPs tell only part of your story. The rest of the story, and often a crucial part, is your personal and professional reputation. Although you are screened or promoted on your record, the path to success lies through the selection board. As we shall see, one or more of the board members briefs your record to the board. At that time, you are discussed, questions are asked, and appraisals are made in open forum by the board. A solid reputation will carry you far in those deliberations. It is rare to have an officer's record go before a promotion or screening board and find that the officer or all of his former skippers are unknown to all of the board members. It is so rare that the unfortunate officer is sometimes referred to as the "mystery person" when this record is briefed to the board. Your reputation started building when you were a midshipman or officer candidate.

Hopefully, you will find that most early mistakes are overlooked with the passage of time. Your seniors, contemporaries, and juniors refine their assessments over time. What do you want them to say about you at wardroom gatherings, in selection and screening board proceedings, and in conversations with your future boss? Just as professional performance is built block by block, so too is your reputation. The deeper consideration is—what matters more to you—what your service jacket records or what others think about you. Unfortunately, I know of officers promoted or given commands because their FITREPs made them "walk on water" despite a contrary reputation. Hopefully, with the insight and preparation that are presented here, the service jacket and FITREPs properly reflect the good reputation that you have earned.

There is an added but not central benefit to a good service reputation. When you do retire, you will carry your service reputation with you. If you have a good reputation, you will be a welcome addition to ship or squadron reunions. You have joined a band of brothers and sisters as you relive the exploits of your youth. At such times your reputation becomes even more precious. But there is more. You will find that your post-service employers in civilian life will also be interested in your military reputation. They do not have access to your fitness reports. But from online sources and ways that will seem mysterious, your prospective employers have their own sources to plumb your reputation during your service years. In some cases, such inputs have been crucial—for good and ill—to the employment decision.[2]

The lesson for junior officers is this. Do not for a minute think that your service reputation is unimportant—even if you are planning to leave the service at your first opportunity. Your service experience will add up to four to six years of your life. You will form or firm up habits during that period that will last a lifetime, both in service and beyond. Future employers will be intensely curious about what you did and how well. Many will not accept a four- to six-year gap in your résumé without some fill-in details. You should view each and every one of your bosses as a person who someday may be asked to comment on your service performance. How would you like to be remembered?

Before getting into the additional considerations of what others might say about you, take a minute to consider the positive attributes that define your family, friends, and associates. And looking in the mirror is a way to consider if you are living up to your own standards and expectations. Be aware that in your naval service, everyone is watching, all the time, and according to Benjamin Franklin, "It takes many good deeds to build a good reputation, and only one bad one to lose it."[3]

4

WHAT SHOULD THEY *NOT* BE SAYING ABOUT YOU?

Your reputation is a priceless asset; guard it zealously. Do not succumb to any act which has the possibility to destroy in an instant the respectability you have earned over a lifetime.
—Rafael C. Benitez, *Anchors: Ethical and Practical Maxims*[1]

To this point in the book, I have emphasized what you should do, not what you should avoid. This chapter emphasizes professional performance and reputation but reverses the perspective and present sketches that serve as cautionary tales. In most cases, these culprits are self-absorbed officers who are having difficulty relating their performance and demeanor to accomplishing their unit's mission. Warren Bennis asserted that you will know leadership when you see it . . . and the negative may be equally true: you will know poor leadership when you see it. And Benjamin Franklin and Rafael Benitez present the reality that your reputation is fragile, and your day-to-day professional and personal performance requires the awareness and strength of character to do and say what is right . . . regardless.

What follows is a series of caricatures of officers with recognizable flaws in their attitudes and performance. You may have already encountered some midshipmen or cadets who at least in part fit these descriptions, and some who have gone on to get a commission. Should you encounter such officers in your unit, the question will be whether you allow them to influence the culture of the unit or whether the strength of the unit will be enough to change their attitudes and behavior. Be self-reflective of how your personal response and behavior can make a difference here.

I suspect you will observe the preponderance of the Navy's officers are hardworking, goal-oriented performers who are good shipmates. But there are limits to how many officers can be above average by any relative standard. Most will not qualify as future CNOs, but they will be competent watch standers, division officers, shiphandlers, and aviators. It is that influential minority that I highlight here, the ones you probably would not depend on in a pinch or welcome as members of the family. Some of them are your competitors in the career race. Some of them will remain in the Navy and be very able and competent indeed.

Years ago, a popular descriptive term was "wardroom lizards"— officers who spend most of their time in the wardroom drinking coffee, shooting the breeze, reading magazines, or even taking a nap. They are rarely out on the deck plates seeing what is going on in their division. The good part of this situation is that their division chief or one of their Sailors with a chit to get signed knows where to find them when needed. By the way, speaking of signing papers, you will soon observe that much of the paperwork (it is not all electronic yet) on a small ship or squadron gets done in the wardroom or ready room. Either no department office exists, or it is so small there is scant room for a junior officer. You have already found out that your stateroom aboard ship is unspeakably small. It is not uncommon to see working papers laid out on the wardroom's table cover and an officer hard at work going over official documents or working with a laptop. These folks are not wardroom lizards; they are trying to get the unit's work done.

The aviation equivalent of wardroom lizards are the squadron mates who believe they came into the Navy only to fly airplanes and that their ground duties are best left to the chief—or department head. When ashore, these officers also seem to be absent a great deal—running errands to the nearby exchange, picking up a latte at the nearby "roach coach," or kicking back in the ready room. You will often be so busy in your naval career you may believe there is never enough time to do what needs to be done. Still, there are lulls when there is time to catch up. Use this time effectively to improve your professional performance: get to know your equipment and spaces better, get to know your enlisted people better, and ensure your time is fully invested. Do not get the reputation as a lounger, an officer who is more comfortable at idling speed than at cruising or top speed.

Some officers do stay very busy, at cruising or top speed. But the unfortunate fact is that they are "all RPM but low output." They give the appearance of staying busy, dashing about with a handful of papers and worried looks on their faces. But for some reason, they do not seem to get anything tangible done. Unfortunately, there is a great deal of administrative work in the peacetime Navy. If you are not careful, it will cloud your judgment. Never forget why you are a naval officer: to be able to operate your ship or squadron effectively in combat. The administration has to get done—and it will be done. And you must do your share. But if most of your working day is spent following social media or reading and responding to email, you (and perhaps your boss) are losing sight of the object of the exercise. Spending your entire day focused on your computer (or phone) screen raises suspicion on how well you are investing your time.

You need to maintain what aviators call "SA" (situational awareness). That is, you need to know how your personal and work environments relate to the big picture, mentally prioritize what you must do, and be very sensitive to changes. True, your work priorities are largely determined by your bosses, but there remains a wedge of time and mental capability under your personal purview. Invest that precious asset wisely.

Some officers personify doom and gloom. The "moaners" see the unit is going to hell in a handbasket, the senior officers do not know what they are doing, and "this old bucket will fall apart if they don't start paying attention." The whiners or complainers are a variant of these moaners. It does not take these types long to deflect their negative outlook upward through the chain of command. The implication is that they are the only ones who know what is really going on—and that others do not know or do not care. These officers never met a job, a duty station, a mission, a boss, or a cruise that they liked and respected. Most are past converting to a more positive outlook. In future years, they will be moaning about why they were not selected or why they were denied the good jobs. A variant of moaners are the officers who severely criticize their subordinates. They seem bemused by their difficulties and are puzzled when asked what their responsibility is for the chaos that swirls around them. These officers live on an island, incompetence above them and beneath them as they sail into the sunset and their first failure before a promotion board.

Rules and regulations are in place for a reason, and there are some individuals who cannot and will not move from the approved guidance to solve a perplexing or new problem. They see compromise as the worst of all evils. They will stubbornly take a position or attitude because, in their words, "it is right." These officers cavil at every suggestion of flexibility or compromise entered into by their bosses to get the job done. Doctrinal or administrative purity is more important than the mission. They pose the false choice that "I would rather be right and passed over than wrong and promoted." A stubborn, inflexible, and self-righteous mindset defines this officer type. While there are absolute rules and regulations for the safe operation of systems in much of what we do in the Navy, there are many areas where the only priority is sound judgment and doing the right thing. When presented with new and unusual circumstances, the moralist can be a real obstacle for those who are trying to get the job done and recognize that there is more than one way to do it.

"Opportunism" is not necessarily a vice. It depends on how it is used. "Striking while the iron is hot," finding "a window of opportunity," and realizing when "the time is right" are all useful admonitions and descriptors. But some individuals exploit opportunity for personal gain and preferment. When they justify an action, you must look carefully for the hidden message. They are slippery, looking for their chance, and often found rooting around in the debris of others' little disasters or periods of chaos. For example, they may be quick to see a trip that is justified on the basis of government business as an opportunity to get a little personal business done at the same time. They may see social functions as opportunities to grind a personal axe with the boss. They see an opportunity to jump in and offer services when a colleague has faltered. In short, they are motivated by self-interest, and in their eyes the mission of the command and its officers is to help them achieve their own objectives. These officers tend to be quick-witted and often are very able. They are dangerous competitors in the face of gullible bosses. Your response to such "ambulance chasing" officers must be predicated on strength and respect, not weakness and venality. Do not cultivate them, but do not accept their self-serving arguments either.

The "gossips" do not seem to accept the simple adage that "loose lips sink ships." It is more than just a security issue, but unprofessional and hazardous to the morale and welfare of a command. Of course, some officers in every unit keep their ears very close to the ground. Little goes on in the command that they do not know. Their pastime is exchanging tidbits with other like-minded souls. They do little harm in most cases, but they foster an atmosphere of greater reserve in social interactions. There is a prevalent fear that private matters will enter the public domain. This is particularly true in the case of misfortunes—who stumbled and why. With the prevalence of social media and ready access to email, all crew members must be cautious of what is being said of the command and the personnel. Think hard before you hit "send" or post.

Closely akin to gossip is loose talk. In this kind of conversation, derogatory information is presented with only a casual regard for—and perhaps ignorance of—the facts. The message is considered more important than its factual basis. But one of the characteristics of your reputation that should be most treasured is that you speak from facts or, when necessary, identify assertions as opinions or allegations. One of the least complimentary things to be said about an officer is that the person acts before thinking, jumps to conclusions, or does not have the facts right.

Following an accident, incident, or otherwise uncertain situation, these gossipers can be very problematic within the command. A simple rule, and for addressing an audience, during a stressful or uncertain time is to be ready with the preface "I will tell you what I know to be true." Such a position limits speculation and gives you the opportunity to come back once you have researched and uncovered the truth.

Some wardrooms or ready rooms have an officer who might be called "too cool for school." These officers are seemingly unperturbed by what is going on around them, have a sardonic detachment from the affairs of the command, seem always to land on their feet, and stay somewhat removed from daily problems and concerns. Officers who are closer to the action and suffer the "slings and arrows of outrageous fortune" often admire these individuals. They seemingly do not care whether the command sinks or swims or succeeds or fails so long as events leave them alone to laugh at lesser mortals embroiled in the fray.

Ordinarily, these officers are not a concern—except when they become ringleaders for officers who want to emulate them. If enough officers take on these individuals' attitudes, the ship or squadron starts to lose its cohesion. The CO or XO who is not alert soon finds that a new power center has been created outside their chain of command. Cliques form, and some are left out—including some of the most diligent and responsible (but perhaps socially inept) officers in the command. It is not your job to save these officers from themselves, but you should be wary of their seductive charm in luring the less sophisticated to their banner.

For "life-of-the-party officers," wardroom and ready room life revolves around partying and horseplay. They are in the forefront of every wild idea, caper, prank, or overseas liberty. Their natural habitat is the "admin" of the unit in every liberty port. If there is no admin, they establish an informal meeting and partying point. Life-of-the-party individuals have most of the organizing and leadership skills needed in a naval officer, leavened with an irreverent sense of humor. They are fun to be around but, in many cases, badly need a rudder or brake to keep them on course. Their stock in trade is the well-placed jibe, the apt phrase, a poke in the ribs, and the riotous takeoff on the characteristics of their seniors and more vulnerable contemporaries. Everybody seems to know them—and their reputation goes beyond the command. Most need a good solid dose of

What Should They *NOT* Be Saying About You?

maturity. As a junior officer, do not mistake life-of-the-party officers as solid performers. Enjoy their company now, because they likely will not be around for a full career unless they gain maturity from the necessary course corrections.

The Navy is a sociable service. For the most part, naval officers and their families enjoy each other's company. The reason for this is shared experiences, often under difficult conditions, and the comradeship that comes from a mission that is larger than any one individual. But there is something more: a sense of loyalty that seems to grow up from the deck plates. Good officers—and most are—and their families help one another.

But some officers are "loners." They enjoy their own company more than that of their shipmates. The possible reasons for this separateness are many. Some are just shy and afraid of rebuke. They are uncomfortable in interpersonal relations. Perhaps they are socially awkward or worried about fitting in. Others are so wrapped up in their own personal interests that they do not have or make the time for community and command interests. They show up and contribute at "command functions" and then go home and are not seen again until quarters the next morning. They keep their own counsel (not bad in itself) and often have to be prodded to become involved with group professional matters. Still others are bookish—introverted scholars whose interests are on an entirely different plane than those of their shipmates.

As a junior officer, you have two obligations in this Navy community. First, do not become or be seen as a loner. Make the effort to become involved in the social life of the command. Take every opportunity to interact with your shipmates in both the professional and social spheres. This is not always easy, and you must be prepared for some rebuffs, but the effort is what counts, and you will likely see that effort reciprocated. Most naval officers are outgoing.

They enjoy comradeship, like to have a good time, and have a sense of humor. They will take it as a matter of pride to draw you out if you are experiencing difficulties in adjusting to the service. For most, their first response is to be inclusive rather than exclusive. Additionally, the enlisted in your division or squadron will want you to be "present"—a term that means more than just physically there, but approachable and interested in their professional and personal life.

Your second obligation is the mirror image of the first: help those who are having trouble making the adjustment to wardroom or ready room comradeship. Making that extra effort pays enormous dividends not only for your new friend but also for your own self-confidence in being able to interact effectively with people who are less self-confident than you are.

The Navy wardroom and ready room are critical places for building a cohesive and capable warfighting command. The collection of officers must, despite the differences in background, ability, and personality, learn to operate with a mission-focused mindset. This chapter introduces some of the personality idiosyncrasies that make this effort easier—or harder. Your reflection on this chapter should give you pause to consider what your reputation is and how you are personally contributing to the welfare of the command.

As you think about how you want to be perceived and how others actually see you, consider a quote attributed to Ralph Waldo Emerson: "What you do speaks so loudly that I cannot hear what you say." Being an officer in the Navy is a 24/7/365 obligation, and you are always "on watch" with the whole world watching.

5

LEVELING THE PLAYING FIELD

Mentor: Trusted counselor or guide
—*Webster's New Collegiate Dictionary*

Coach: A support and guide for the coaching partner's goals
—*MyNavy Coaching*

Clique: A narrow exclusive circle or group
—*Webster's New Collegiate Dictionary*

We utilize a compass as one of the most important instruments in navigation. The objective of this edition of *Career Compass* is to achieve the goal of a successful Navy career, and the chapters provide the additional insight and direction to navigate the charted career paths and to point you to the resources that keep you on course and out of the shoals. We all enter the Navy from differing backgrounds, commissioning sources, and life experiences, with differing expectations and goals for our military career and life in general. This chapter highlights some of the perceived differences from your entry into the Navy and suggests tools that should level the field in competition for promotion and command in your chosen warfare area.

In the military, industry, and academia, there is a growing interest and investment in mentoring and coaching programs. The intent is to commit the time and resources to develop individuals (at all levels) personally and professionally to help attain their goals and those of the institution or corporation. While neither are official Navy programs, mentoring has been readily valued over the years for personal career development, and MyNavy Coaching is a recent initiative that has the same end in mind but takes a differing approach to the process.[1]

The basic difference between mentoring and coaching lies in how the mentor or coach engages with the mentee or the coaching partner in the development process. The mentor's approach is, "You will learn from my experiences; I will tell you what you should do." Coaches, on the other hand, say, "You will learn from our experiences; I will ask you what you hope to accomplish."

Mentors

Mentoring involves a senior-junior relationship based on advice, friendship, and mutual respect and in some cases an extension of influence on the part of the senior. In the naval service, this relationship has mostly been informal and limited within a particular warfare area. At their best, mentors provide a channel of career advice from an interested senior to a junior. At worst, mentoring may involve a senior using influence to gain some preferment (assignment or selection) for the junior outside the system.

Mentors can enhance their mentee's service reputation in a variety of ways. For example, in their conversations with other senior officers, mentors might mention something about their protégé's superior performance. This information might be particularly useful to those seniors shopping to fill an important billet on their staffs. Most influence involves passing the word on the good qualities of a mentee. In that sense, it is a positive component of one's service reputation. Nevertheless, some believe this type of mentoring is a form of political influence. I see it otherwise. Service reputation is a fact of life, and it is naive to suggest that it be eliminated from the most sensitive decisions the Navy makes—that is, officer assignments and promotions.

The most valuable service a mentor can provide is career advice. This advice goes far beyond such matters as future assignments. It includes guidance and suggesting how to perform in staff and command functions, setting an example for the junior to emulate, pointing out the pitfalls and opportunities as one progresses in a naval career, and exposing the mentee to the real issues of the Navy that lie beyond the command's routine.

In today's environment, it behooves you to have someone you would call a mentor—someone who is accessible, like-minded, and interested in your success (which might be defined by their success). It is not a contract and is rarely mentioned in specific terms. An engaging mentor works with you because they see promise in you and they want to help you realize it. They, like you, are willing to invest the time to share experience and expectations. It is an extension of friendship in the professional realm—and, like friendship, it has to this point stayed informal. In fact, the word "mentor" is rarely used. You might hear a senior say, "He is one of my boys," "I have been following her career closely," "He bears watching," or "She has great potential." Or a junior may jokingly refer to their mentor as a "sea daddy."

This is all well and good, but if this is not a "program," how can you be more proactive in coming to the attention of senior officers and thereby obtaining some of the benefits of having a mentor? At the Naval Academy, as the midshipmen are deciding what career field they should pursue, and more specifically after service assignment, they are highly encouraged to seek out a mentor who can fill in their specific career information gaps.[2] As part of a required practicum course (once service assignments are made), junior officers in the mentor role provide helpful hints for getting off to a good start in their first and qualifying tours. This highlights a difference in opportunity between the Naval Academy and other commissioning sources that have limited access to the pool of fleet officers who are readily available for meetings and classes. The one encouragement is to make the most of the summer training evolutions and be proactive in communicating with the officers you might meet during them. In the fleet and after commissioning, the opportunity for building a mentor relationship will not be as structured, and the initiative to build a mentor relationship then will fall on you. Who do you see within your command or warfare area who demonstrates the character, personality, and warfare savvy that you wish to emulate? Are you prepared to express your interest and commit your time to invest in the relationship, with good questions and clear personal career objectives? A seasoned mentor will not appreciate the request to "please teach me all you know about (a topic)." They will want the time to be spent addressing thoughtful questions, the responses to which will rely on personal experience and understanding of current and future community issues.

If the thought of asking someone senior to commit their time and energy concerns you, the good news is that you do have one powerful tool readily at your disposal: superior performance in your current job. You will come to the attention of both your commanding officer and other potential mentors if you are demonstrating sustained superior performance. The word spreads quickly. Additionally, you will find that there are very few successful officers who cannot instantly list the mentors that have helped them along the way. Theirs is a commitment to pay it forward within their community. When you succeed, your boss succeeds, and career-minded officers will not be shy about helping you with advice to a successful career.[3]

At the end of a successful tour, when your mentor says, "This is what you should do next," you know you are tracking!

Coaches

Coaching takes a very different approach to the mentor senior-junior relationship, and may even be a peer-to-peer connection. As outlined in MyNavy Coaching, it is less important that I know the requirements and gates to get you to your desired goal, but more important that I can ask the open-ended questions that cause you (and me) to consider the opportunities, challenges, and issues approaching those goals. Coaching is seen as a tool that can improve one's interpersonal skills of interactive listening, empathy, asking powerful questions, and encouragement. Unlike a mentor, the coach should avoid giving answers or advice. Doing so may remove the independence of the coaching partner and may even lead to solving the wrong problem. Like mentoring, the strength of the coaching partnership depends on the commitment of both parties to the coaching partner's success by facilitating learning, improving performance, and moving toward the desired results. Partnering in coaching (and mentoring) requires a level of trust and commitment on behalf of the coach and the coaching partner.

While many of the top universities are advertising programs to become certified executive coaches, the Navy (for now) promotes the benefits of coaching, not as a graduate degree program, but as a career and life skill builder that can better develop you as a leader and attract and retain the best talent for the Navy.[4] Utilizing the principles of the GROW (goal, reality, options, and will) model to frame coaching questions will necessarily help both parties develop better communication and relational skills.[5] Because such a large part of leadership in the Navy includes counseling and assessment, the practiced attributes exercised in coaching will certainly benefit any aspiring leader and their organization.

What advice can I offer on these subjects? Consider what would best help you in pursuit of your goals. A coach, by asking strong questions, may help you resolve conflicts or concerns you have when making particular life and career decisions. Once a clear goal is established, a mentor with the background and experience might be best able to steer you along the desired path. Regardless, within the Navy there is a community of experts who want for you to be satisfied and successful—for you, for our Navy, for our nation.

If you are a senior, show interest in the success of subordinates, and see if that grows into a relationship based on mutual respect and friendship. Make yourself available to mentor or coach others. Either is for their good and benefit, not as an obligation to show favor or circumvent the established evaluation and promotion systems. As a junior, mentoring and/or coaching may or may not come to you, but it is recommended that you engage in the opportunities. If it does come to you, be careful not to abuse a confidence or friendship or seek preferment outside existing systems (the word gets out). Be open, honest, and respectful of your coach or mentor's time and effort. Your best current mentor may be your commanding officer because that officer has official levers with which to help and counsel you. Commanding officers can talk to detailers and placement officers, and they sign your fitness reports. They know your strengths and weaknesses and can advise you based on a factual observation of your performance. In fact, many mentorships start out as skipper–junior officer relationships.

At the end of a successful tour, your coach will ask what you hope to do next in the near and long term . . . and may quickly shift the mentor hat to tell you what you need to do next—all good advice for you to consider.

Cliques

The discussion so far concerning those who are interested in supporting you in your career and life aspirations has focused on one-on-one relationships with like-minded individuals, some senior, some junior, and some your peers. There is, however, a special type of group mentorship or collegiality that may be detrimental to you and to Navy good order and discipline: cliques. Destructive cliques (with some of the attributes highlighted in chapter 4) can be a form of abusive mentorship and cronyism in your organization. Unfortunately, the histories of the armed services, including the Navy, suggest instances where a small group of officers may have attempted to manipulate the promotion and assignment systems to the advantage of themselves and favored colleagues. In some cases, such cronyism was defended as advancing the good of the service. It was rarely overtly venal or self-serving. Indeed, the usual rationale for group cohesion was based on loyalty and forming a "team" or informal association to achieve some worthwhile end.[6] Unfortunately, carrying interpersonal loyalty and team building to the extreme works against the larger officer population who are not included among the "in" groups. Even the best of motives can carry one too far, and fairness and equity are sacrificed to achieve a personal objective.

The point is that the extent of the benefits of building relationships as a mentor or coach must be metered. Knowing that a person is "one of my boys," or that I am "following her career closely" must not be used to subvert the chain of command or for giving any individual or group preferment or special access to important decision-makers or friends. Hold the enthusiasms for the individuals in check. The key is to keep your perspective and balance, be wary of "countercultures" brewing within the command, and be reminded that our loyalty to the Navy should not be confused with loyalty to an individual or group, no matter how strong.

The Naval Academy Connection

Much has been made over the years about the bigger fraternity and supposed bonding that Naval Academy graduates enjoy and the assumed advantages they have over officers commissioned from other sources. Some of this criticism loses its punch when one considers the current makeup of their wardroom or ready room, and the bios of recent CNOs and future COs and XOs. The Naval Academy commissions about one-third of the Navy officers each year, and the promotion rates through the ranks do not support the claim of unfair advantage.[7]

Let me be clear here: the Naval Academy is here for a reason—to produce career officers and leaders for the nation and to set the standard for officer-producing systems throughout the service. The facts show that Naval Academy graduates have a higher career retention rate than do graduates of other commissioning programs. That is not the same as saying that other systems produce less qualified officers. Nor is it to say that Naval Academy graduates enjoy any head start benefits throughout their careers. Nor is it to say that Naval Academy graduates are not proud alumni who have a bond of shared experience with other graduates that remains throughout their lifetime.

There is one special advantage—not crucial, but important—of a Naval Academy education. While midshipmen are at the Naval Academy, they come into contact with seven classes of midshipmen (their own class when they enter the academy, the three classes in front of them, and the three classes that follow as they progress). They graduate in sequence and then march through their careers together. It follows that graduates know the strengths and weaknesses of a large part of the officer corps at any given time starting with their own commissioning. They enter the fleet with a very large professional acquaintance among their contemporaries. This translates to the fact that their professional reputations, for good or ill, are more widely known in the service than those of their non–Naval Academy contemporaries. While the Naval Academy's staff and military professors are heavily weighted with Naval Academy graduates, the large addition of non-Academy officers (ranks O-3 to O-6) provides a regular dose of reality that reduces any sense of superiority or advantage. Hence, midshipmen at the Naval Academy graduate with an exposure to a large number of officers, with a broad spectrum of experience beyond their own or adjacent year groups or Naval Academy background.

Although the Naval Academy provides excellent preparation for lifelong service in the naval profession, it demonstrably is not the only way for professional success and the promotions that go with it. I have served with, under, and over officers from all accession sources. It would never occur to me, or anybody I know, to give preferment to Naval Academy graduates simply because they were graduates of that institution. Any CO wants the best people regardless of commissioning source. To imply that there is some "canoe club" or "boat school" or "ring knocker" service mentality that stands in the way of promotion of nongraduates is not valid. Although it may have had some basis up to and through World War II, that practice has long been dead. The Navy has changed from being led by a force of some five thousand Naval Academy–trained officers in the 1930s to one of more than fifty thousand officers from a variety of commissioning sources today. Even if it wanted to, the Naval Academy cannot supply all or even most of the service's officer needs.

For a number of years, I taught a leadership course at OCS in Newport where a routine question from candidates was, "How can I compete with the Naval Academy graduates?" I found that the academy advantage was mostly familiarity with terminology and tradition. Because of the four-year routine and the extensive summer training, the academy graduates had a head start in this regard, which was quickly erased by the junior officers who applied themselves professionally and leaned on their many (and important) life experiences in dealing with the challenges of shipboard duty. Do not focus on any initial edge that a Naval Academy graduate may have on commissioning. Hard work and sustained superior performance will make anyone competitive, regardless of the commissioning source.

6

SPRING TRAINING

> Chance favors the prepared mind.
>
> —Louis Pasteur

Every spring, the attention of baseball fans is drawn toward Florida and Arizona as favorite teams undertake spring training and prepare for the upcoming baseball season. At this time, players hone the skills needed to perform throughout a season that for some does not end until the following October. Getting physically and mentally in shape for an uncertain future is not limited to ballplayers, however. For naval officers, spring training is actually a year-round activity: getting ready for the next position, the next hurdle, and the challenges of leadership in an environment where the stakes are much higher than on the baseball diamond.

How do you prepare yourself to achieve good performance and, ultimately, promotion? A better question is, how do you prepare yourself to perform at a higher level? The answer reads like a menu, where your best results come from selecting and applying all the entrées. Achieving some of the skills needed requires—surprise!—hard work and continued application. In this chapter are some techniques that should get your attention.

Mentally Fleeting Up

"Fleeting up" is a time-honored Navy term that describes taking over your boss's job when that individual is not there. But the fleeting-up concept is also a useful technique for preparing yourself for command. Using this method, you simply contemplate the decision your boss is called on to make and then mentally put yourself in his or her place and work the problem through to a solution. This is not the time for glib comments or jocular guesses. Make this effort only if you do it seriously, as there are no simple answers to the major problems of command.

A variant of this technique is to assume your boss has become incapacitated (the "what if they were hit by a bus?" scenario) and that now it is up to you to make the necessary decisions. Imagine that your professional reputation rests on the decision. You must act! This vicarious mode of decision-making and learning will expand your mind, and you will grow both in situational awareness and in preparedness. What would be your agenda if you suddenly had to represent your ship or squadron in discussions with your skipper's commodore or carrier air wing commander? Put aside the conventional wisdom of your junior officer buddies. For the moment, even if only in your mind, assume you are wearing your boss's stripes and that what you do will have a major influence on your command. Have you done the hard preparatory work—spring training—of marshaling the facts and working the problem?

In Navy aviation, and now more in the surface warfare community, the XO is assigned to a command with the intention of taking command after eighteen to twenty-four months. This "left seat–right seat" concept comes from the principle that the pilot is in the left seat and the copilot (trainee or student) is in the right seat. The eventual progression is to move to the left seat. In the term of being the XO, the officer learns the ship, the crew, and the operational requirements. The expectation is that they will be mentally "fleeting up" continuously as they know that they will soon be in the CO's seat. While the principle is basically baked into the XO's orders, the idea has great practicality for all officers. If you are ever concerned about what "they" are doing and ordering, remember you are part of "they" and that you should be considering how you would be making the change and the orders.

As a creative suggestion for commanding officers: Give your XO and department heads the day off and tell your junior officers that they will fill the temporarily vacant positions for the day (let your commodore or air wing commander know what is going on). Your junior officers should prepare and sign off on the plan of the day, the flight schedule, and the messages that must be sent. If this prospect worries you, you should ask yourself what you are doing to prepare them to fill the gaps when the need arises. When the first team returns, call a wardroom/ready room meeting and ask how your junior officers improved on the example their seniors have set. This exercise gives you and them an opportunity to make some serious points from which all can benefit.

Within the regular shipboard refresher training of the ship's schedules, this can become a forced element in the evaluation. The training team may suddenly announce that the top watch stander or team leader is incapacitated and the assessment of your readiness depends on how well the watch/response teams fleet up to continue to fight the ship. Consider how deep you can go with qualified personnel to make critical command decisions.

Focusing on Where Your Command Needs the Most Help

Adm. Ernest King, the Navy's CNO during World War II, once remarked, "'Difficulties' is the name given to things it is our business to overcome."[1] As you look around you, what are your command's "difficulties" or problems? What can be done about them? What can you do to help your department head or skipper? Look at problems as a puzzle to be solved, not a difficulty to be avoided. Put a list of such problems on your computer and keep a running commentary on solutions—those you offer and those that are actually affected by your bosses. As a chief engineer, this was a valuable tool for me to keep focused on longer-term issues and was also an end-of-tour reflection of what had actually been accomplished and what I was leaving as action for my relief.

For example, let us suppose your command has a shortage of personnel in a few important ratings. Consider the command's billet structure and how it is manned (what the command is allowed and what it has on board). Add in when more personnel are expected. Ask yourself what levers the command has to gain improvement. What workarounds are available? What messages would you send, and what discussions would you have with your commodore or air wing commander or the Navy Personnel Command? How would you make the onboard personnel more effective? What will be the effects if the shortfall is not remedied before deployment? Or, to expand your examination further afield, why is that rating so chronically undermanned? What are the selective reenlistment bonuses or special pay levels for the ratings in question? How can the Navy offer more than the civilian job market? How can mentoring or coaching tools help in the development and retention arenas? Thinking above your pay grade is a valuable exercise to get you ready for the XO or a Navy Personnel Command position.

Speaking Up and Speaking Out

Are you taking advantage of every opportunity to polish your public speaking skills? One such opportunity is holding training sessions with your division. Surely you know something that they need to know in order to do well on promotion exams. If you avoid opportunities to hone your communications skills before an audience, you are postponing the inevitable. If you aspire to command, you will be required to speak in public and speak well.

At the Naval Academy, the midshipmen attend a regular rotation of mandatory presentations. The groans are audible when one more distinguished speaker is added to their evening agenda. My less than sympathetic response to their displeasure is: "Tomorrow I want you to tell me: what was the main message from the speaker, and how well did they present that message?" While the assignment is a forcing function to pay attention, it is intended to have the midshipmen consider how they should speak to a very critical audience. Should I use notes? Is it okay to read my notes? What is an introductory story to connect to the crowd? What signal does my body language send? Are my jokes relevant? Does everyone understand my acronyms? How long can I hold their attention? Did I leave the audience with any nuggets of advice and help? The list of questions goes on, but the results are for the midshipmen to consider the smallest aspects of public speaking, which will determine the impact of their message. They practice with their classmates, but it will be game on when they are in front of a division, department, or squadron.

The second part of this section is the speaking out. A humble boss will cherish the subordinate who can address problems or leadership concerns within the command. Who is willing to tell the emperor they have no clothes? It takes courage to speak up to a boss when you see something is amiss. The first important point is that you recognize there is a problem; second, is there something that you can do to remediate it; and finally, can you bring it to the boss in a helpful way. Not all bosses are clear in their intentions, some don't want to hear bad news, and not all bosses want to hear dissention to their plans.

Practice being the boss that communicates well, can be approached, is willing to listen, and, when appropriate, admits to being wrong (or might have been wrong!). Like so many other good things, however, speaking well takes work and practice. Always be ready to speak up and speak out!

Knowing the Most About the Systems

Who in your unit knows the most about the systems under your cognizance? Your first answer to this question is probably your chief petty officer, which is an understandable response, particularly if you have not been aboard very long. But how far down the enlisted rate structure in your division do you have to go before your knowledge is on a par? When you determine that level, ask yourself what value *you* contribute to your division's "product." Have you ever studied the advancement in rate manuals that apply to the ratings in your division? Could you pass the exam? If not, why not? Do you see your role as solely an officer in training and, hence, excused from the need to acquire concrete and fundamental knowledge of the system? If you do see your role that way, when do you believe that circumstance will change? If you remain unconcerned about the details of the work under your cognizance, you will not make it—not in the Navy and not in civilian life. There is no easy path from where you stand today to achieving an intimate knowledge of the content of the job and ultimately becoming an executive or leader who can instruct others. The ladder is slippery, and each rung on the way up is hard earned and easily measured.

The tenor and content of these questions and comments should suggest to you that you need to be hands-on with what is going on in the division or in matters under your cognizance. Skating along and giving excuses ("Let the chief do it") are easy. Ambitious officers who are preparing themselves for command put aside the easy way and are hands-on performers who know their "stuff." This does not mean that you do the chief's work for that individual. Chiefs have their jobs to do, and you should stay out of their business (business that usually centers on the "how," not necessarily the "what" or "when"). But basic professional competence is both their business and yours.

In the operational and maintenance cycle of ships, subs, and aircraft, there are numerous opportunities to learn (from system experts) more of the specifications of the system that you operate. The Board of Inspection and Survey (INSURV) was a very important shipboard schoolhouse for me in my initial division officer assignment.[2] Operationally stressing all of the engineering equipment, then disassembling, inspecting, and reassembling it (with INSURV members on-site) gave me the internal look at the machinery in my spaces, and an assessment of the technical skills of my Sailors. The point is that when an assist (or inspection) team comes to your command, or you are in an availability for maintenance or upgrades, be in the hip pocket of the technicians, installers, inspectors, and testers. They are there because of their expertise, and the job for you and your Sailors is to glean as much as possible from them.

Peace to War

How would your job (and your attitude toward it) change if we went to war tomorrow? Considering this topic is another way of clearing out the peacetime cobwebs. So much of what we do in peacetime is oriented to administering, saving operating funds, taking care of our equipment, and training that we often overlook priorities directly related to warfighting. Suppose survival and warfighting took place over your peacetime maintenance and training missions—and your prospects of advancement. This type of spring cleaning is occasionally needed in every command except those actually in combat or on the verge of deployment to a combat theater. Have you thought of proposing to your skipper that you orchestrate and direct an internal exercise for your unit to establish a warfighting mindset? Make the general quarters drills as real as possible! Make sure everyone in the command knows their role or potential role. Be ready to do more than damage control; be ready to continue fighting—and fighting well.

Focusing on Physical Fitness

To those who have been in combat or extreme weather conditions, one of the most vivid memories is not fear but the physical exhaustion occasioned by long stretches of stress, anxiety, and uncertainty. We all have experienced (or will experience) the long periods on the bridge, in the cockpit, or in ready status on the catapult preparing a series of weapons launches, performing underway replenishments, and looking for the enemy while ensuring the unit stays in a high state of readiness. We have all had situations where at any moment we might have to give our best to survive and complete the mission. As far back as World War I, the naval service at war was described as "months of boredom punctuated by moments of terror."[3]

Although there is a large portion of mental preparedness in this equation, physical readiness is of vital importance as well. Are you in shape? Can you function in an environment of long periods of sleep deprivation? Once you get out of shape, it becomes increasingly difficult with age to regain it. When you step on the bridge, go into combat, or drop in the cockpit, you should be rested and alert. But you must work to achieve the conditions that make it possible. Physical fitness is one of the best assets you can have in the professional performance sweepstakes. You need not be a varsity athlete—but you must have strength, stamina, and adequate rest. You need to manage your physical condition the same way you would manage any other asset. This means proper diet (when possible), the ability to catch catnaps on the fly during the rare interludes, and exercise.

In the British navy, there is an enlisted rating for physical training instructor (*clubs*, in slang).[4] Their responsibility is supervising the mandatory continuous fitness program for the command. In the U.S. Navy, the roles of command fitness leader and assistant command fitness leader are collateral duties for some interested Sailor or officer who can administer the body composition assessment[5] and the physical readiness test,[6] and organize some command sports teams to compete in local base competitions. So, the specific maintenance of your personal fitness lies with you.

Exercise means more than strength conditioning, although that is important. It also involves aerobic exercise to stress your cardiovascular system, keep your body pipes clean, and keep you alert. If you do not sweat, you are not working out. You also need to ensure that your range of motion is adequate, and that takes exercise also—stressing your arms, legs, torso, and neck in a disciplined way through the limits of your range. But the most important habit is to get into a regular routine of exercise—not crash courses to get back in shape. Your exercise regimen should be designed carefully so that you test and increase your limits without overdoing it; it should also be suitable for use aboard ship and ashore. If your command does not have a regimented schedule for fitness, I would suggest that you consider adding that to the routine planning board for training (PB4T). Do not let daily priorities push aside your need for a routine fitness program. You will not cross the career finish line at the top of your game unless you are in good shape. Nobody else can do it for you. And another observation: many officers encounter health problems as selection board problems as they become more senior. If your health becomes questionable because of diet or lack of exercise, so are your prospects for promotion.

Looking Fit

How do you look? Physical fitness is part of the answer to this question. You must look fit, and you will if you are fit. A round of golf every week simply will not do it. Do not mistake fun for fitness, although there is some overlap. Do your uniforms fit? If not, get in shape so that they do, or get new uniforms. Do you look like an officer your subordinates would follow in battle? Is your uniform clean, pressed, and worn properly? Many observers who do not know your hidden sterling professional qualities will get their initial impression from your appearance in uniform.

Beyond physical condition and dress is the matter of personal demeanor. Current fashion and cultural trends call for tattered jeans and a "casual" shuffle or scuff from one point to another. Some persons find it difficult to maintain eye contact. Others slur their words in imitation of the latest pop group performer or film star. For the new officer, most of these attributes are left behind after plebe summer or during basic training in their OCS or Naval Reserve Officers Training Corps (NROTC) unit. But over a lifetime, you should pay attention to your posture, your grooming, and the smartness of your uniform. Get in the habit of looking a conversation partner square in the eye, sharing a firm handshake, and speaking clearly and directly. If you look alert, involved, and decisive, you probably are, and you will find these attributes serve you well in watch standing and combat.

Figuratively and literally—look at yourself in the mirror regularly (because others will always be looking at you) to determine if you present yourself admirably!

7

DO YOU SHINE IN THE CAREER MARKETPLACE?

> Good performance produces good assignments. High performers don't really get a choice of assignments. On the other hand, they get choice assignments because of their high performance.
> —Vice Adm. Robert F. Dunn, USN (Ret.)

What is it that makes some officers so well known among their peers and seniors? A few officers are tabbed as admiral material while still lieutenant commanders and commanders. One individual that clearly came to my mind was a plebe in my squad at the Naval Academy whom we tabbed to be a future brigade commander (and he was). He followed with exceptional junior officer tours, successful command tours, executive assistant to a four-star, and rose to the position of four-star admiral himself. This was a surprise to no one! Some, probably with a bit of jealousy, refer to these select few as "the favorites," "water walkers," or "the chosen one." Other highly regarded officers are spared such labels but clearly and with some generosity of spirit are considered head and shoulders above their contemporaries.

What is it that clearly marked these officers so early in their careers? Each story has a different key element. One is beloved by his subordinates as a superb tactician, brilliant combat leader, and people-oriented commander. Another is remembered for her intellectual brilliance, her decisiveness, and her ability to get things done in tough environments. Another is still recognized as respected skipper and a tough-minded CNO and chairman of the joint chiefs of staff when major decisions had to be made. Reading the biographies of admirals like Raymond Spruance, Chester Nimitz, Arleigh Burke, James Flatley Jr., Thomas Moorer, Elmo Zumwalt, Michael Mullen, James Stavridis, or Michelle Howard reveals the various paths to four stars, where the consistent theme is commitment to the naval mission and professionally and competently performing well in challenging situations. They all took on the tough jobs on the way up and did them well—so well that they came to the attention of the entire naval service. In some cases, those jobs involved great political skill (and risk), but not political skill in terms of advancing themselves. Instead, they had skill in getting a high-visibility job done under the difficult conditions of working with other naval organizations or warfare specialties and other services. Later in their careers, they worked just as skillfully with other organizations—Congress, the joint chiefs, or diplomatic representatives of the country's allies.

Characteristics of Up-and-Comers

Now step back from the careers of a small number of legendary flag officers and look around you, both within and outside your current command. Some of your contemporaries are already gaining recognition as being "head and shoulders" officers and are well known (at least by reputation) to you as "up-and-comers." What strikes you about their performance? Put luck aside. No one is lucky or unlucky for the twenty to twenty-two years it takes to make captain or to fail for selection one or more times. Some salient characteristics of these officers catch the eye.

When you consider your friends, contemporaries, and seniors who enjoy this status, you will note some common characteristics that stand out. First, you would identify strength of intellect. Even if they are not the smartest people in the race for advancement, they are smart enough to learn quickly from their mistakes and those of others and to see how the lessons apply to often unpredictable future situations. Intellectual acuity and suppleness are key virtues. And you will observe that some of that intellectual ability can be learned along the way. It is not a birthright.

Second, you might observe that they are decisive and have the ability to communicate their decisions and advice in such a way as to be compelling and persuasive to seniors and subordinates. Often this skill is acquired as a very junior officer. In short, they are courageous decision-makers. They are not needless risk-takers, but they know when and how to make a decision and disregard personal consequences. They sail close to the wind, but they are never becalmed. C. S. Forester, a great English naval novelist, had Admiral Lord Sir William Cornwallis cautioning a young Commander Horatio Hornblower: "But remember this. You'll find it hard to perform your duty unless you risk your ship. There's folly and there's foolhardiness on one side, and there are daring and calculation on the other. Make the right choice and I'll see you through any trouble that may ensue."[1]

Third, we would note that the emerging great leaders have the best kind of toughness, even ruthlessness, to make the correct decision regardless of personal consequences. Their critics may add that the ruthlessness sometimes extends to their desire to succeed at a personal level. But experience tells us that personally ruthless officers seldom succeed to high command, and when they do, they are heartily disliked and that that dislike feeds back into diminishing their personal reputation and eventually puts a cap on their aspirations.

The better form of ruthlessness puts the highest premium on moral integrity and mission accomplishment. The popular Hollywood stereotype of a very popular commander who puts the affection of his crew as his principal objective misses the mark, and he is not the person I want to lead me in combat. Subordinates prefer the commander who is successful as an operator and in combat. They will brag about this individual endlessly. They expect their skippers to be hard but fair—a phrase that captures the essence of the mental and moral toughness that is so highly regarded.

One naval leader who carried such ruthlessness to the extreme was Adm. Ernest J. King, the CNO during World War II. King did not suffer fools gladly and had little time for friendship. His loyalty was to the service, not to individuals. King was disliked by many, feared by some, but respected by almost all.[2] He had a tough job to do—picking up the pieces after a major naval defeat and going on to win a major war against tenacious and able enemies. One does not have to enjoy King's sundowner's reputation—that is, tough, strong-minded, and ruthless—but all can learn from his single-minded focus on the objective. He harshly pushed aside officers, some very senior, who did not measure up or who were unsuited for combat decision-making, even though they had scaled the promotion ladders of the peacetime Navy. Maybe the additional lesson was the importance of being a subordinate like Nimitz, Spruance, and William Halsey, who were able to understand their bosses' tendencies and reputation and continue to focus on the mission and execute orders in their respective personal manner. There will be times in your career when you will be faced with making what appears to be a ruthless decision, and for the good of the service, it is the right thing to do. This is the leadership Admiral King demonstrated in World War II.

The Marketplace

In this text, the marketplace is not the job market for those ready to pursue some other occupation in industry or government. The marketplace for naval officers is defined by the demand for the *best* officers to be placed in the *best* positions, and the small supply of those officers. Note the emphasis on the word *best*. Many good officers are available to fill billets, but understandably every skipper and shore boss wants the best. They want the best because they view their jobs as deserving the best and because if they have the best working for them, they will do a better job. The battles in the marketplace are joined wherever officer service jackets for key positions are reviewed by selective seniors, during flag-slating sessions conducted at the top levels of the Navy, and in the day-to-day interaction between placement and detailer officers in the Navy Personnel Command. The battles are strongly fought, and at times the officer being considered becomes directly involved. Mostly the battle is fought by others with you as the prize. So, how do you shine in such a Navy marketplace?

It almost goes without saying that the key elements of a top-notch promotion jacket are outstanding fitness reports, commendations, and other bouquets. This book is largely about how you should perform and ultimately build such a performance record. The second ingredient to competitiveness in the marketplace is your professional reputation. This becomes even more critical as you become more senior and the number of your active duty contemporaries decreases. By the time you are a captain, and in some cases as a commander, you will be well known to those who have the biggest voice in your future.

But this record building begins in your present job. By the time you are more senior and have had a very successful major command tour as a captain, you are considered to be a contender for flag rank and are looked over very carefully in the assignment and placement process. You will find that your services are much sought after and that the detailers treat your next assignment very carefully.

A third component is your set of professional credentials. Have you had postgraduate education in the field related to the billet under consideration? For example, do you have a subspecialty in such areas as communications, computer management, or comptrollership? Have you served in joint or combined billets? Have you had a successful command tour? The reality is that the needs of the Navy and demands of the placement officers will continue to shift as the types and capabilities of our Navy platforms change and the political, social, and economic pressures demand more specialized capabilities. The future is uncertain, so sustaining as much flexibility in your résumé may be critical. As a senior detailer in the engineering duty community, I saw the shift to more program managers with financial backgrounds and experience. As an experienced engineer in 1200 PSI super-heated steam plants, I saw the shift to gas turbines and was forlorn when the boiler technician rating was discontinued and maintenance and operations of the limited conventional boiler systems were assigned to machinist mates.

The final element of your marketability is your experience. Do you have recent fleet experience? Have you proved yourself in tough jobs? Have you dealt with Congress, foreign officials, or the civilian departments of government? No one expects all of these credentials and experiences in a junior officer, but they do expect you to fill out your résumé as you grow in seniority. You should have a shopping bag of skills that includes command at sea and a variety of tools earned in command positions ashore. The question is not only how your fitness reports look in the marketplace, but also what else you have to offer.

I have often said I am not comfortable being a salesman, but I realize that I have spent my entire adult life in that sales position. I have been recruiting and retaining enlisted personnel and officers by promoting the importance and benefits of the naval service. And, additionally relevant to this chapter, I have made the continuous effort to ensure my official record was an accurate reflection of my service, and to be honest and open about my accomplishments and aspirations to best position me for the next opportunity and assignment. If I were looking to fill an important position, I hope that I would hire me.

8

BEEN TO SCHOOL LATELY?

> Officers in year group 2015 and beyond will be required to graduate from an in-residence program prior to assuming Major Command.
> —NAVADMIN 263/18 Update to Graduate Education Program

The junior officer reader may be saying, "Whoa! I just got here. Major command is something that commanders and captains worry about." That's true, but if you stay for a career, you will encounter the Navy's schoolhouse again, and the timing, duration, and content of that encounter can affect your assignments, career progression, promotions, and major command. You should start thinking now about your plan to further your education while in the Navy. You should pay careful attention to your detailer's briefs pointing to the timing and duration for education opportunities. You still have time to decide, but careful consideration is needed early in your career as to how school fits with your personal aspirations, family expectations, and community requirements.

The Navy has made the Graduate Education Program a priority to "support our National Defense Strategy by developing Navy leaders who understand the art and science of warfighting and can lead in complex strategic environments." Additionally, the current commitment to in-residence programs recognizes the need for work-life balance and provides the best opportunity for developing "mature critical and/or strategic thinking skills."[1]

The Navy's schoolhouse can be a controversial subject because individuals in leadership positions hold strong but alternative views about how officers should spend their years in the face of competing demands in a fast-paced career. John Paul Jones is recorded as stating a naval officer "should be of a liberal education,"[2] but over the years, many believed that a naval officer's natural school ground was the school of the ship, not the halls of academe. The old salts strongly resisted the establishment of the U.S. Naval Academy. The establishment of the Naval War College and the Naval Postgraduate School (NPS) faced lesser but nonetheless similar opposition. That era is behind us, but the debate over the benefit of graduate-level schooling compared to the experience of line duty remains.

A Navy Education

Four major components make up the Navy's officer education programs: undergraduate programs such as the Naval Academy and the NROTC system; the many schools in the long training pipelines for officers going to billets where education is as important as training; the Navy graduate education program at NPS and selected public and private universities; and professional military education (PME) at the Naval War College and the comparable war and staff college programs of the other services, the joint colleges, and the colleges of some of our international security partners. The discussion that follows centers on the last three components listed.

The Sea Duty Pipeline

The Navy's leadership puts most of its attention and funding on imparting professional technical skills (many such skills have an education component), not on academic scholarship. Accordingly, more emphasis is placed on the officer training pipelines to the fleet than on graduate education programs. These pipelines include nuclear power training and refresher tours, replacement aircrew training, the various surface warfare schools, and assorted sea-oriented schools that prepare you directly for your fleet billet (e.g., engineering schools, catapult and arresting gear schools, missile courses, department head, and the prospective commanding officer schools). The detailers will be sure to make it your priority to get to the right and necessary schools to remain current and proficient. The Navy has not made a conscious decision to trade off higher education for pipeline training, but the effect remains by default.

The importance of performance in these fleet schools should be readily apparent within the community wardrooms. Satisfactory completion of qualification exams and interviews is a necessity, and class standing may have a direct implication on the following duty assignment. Your reputation starts, and continues, with your standing in the Navy schools, which routinely recognize and reward the highest classroom achievers.

Postgraduate Education

Most officers today want an advanced degree but see little time available to get it without risking a detour in their careers. (This is contrary to the expectations for most of the restricted line– and special duty–communities, where the career path requires early advanced education and/or professional certifications for assignment and promotion.) As described in OPNAVINST 1520.23C, "Education is a strategic investment in the development of warfighters," but the consideration of current tactical need and the future strategic investment challenges the priority for an officer's shore tour opportunity.[3] An additional expectation in the CNO's instruction is that the service member "should expect to serve in an educational related billet" following their degree completion. Compliance with this directive is an even more challenging effort for the detailers and the officers. When asked, many of these degree aspirants will frankly admit that they want the degree more for their post-service résumé than for any direct benefit they might see during their naval service. As far as they are concerned, an advanced degree (particularly in a liberal arts or business field) is a plus for them, but not a key ingredient in the deliberations of future assignments or a future selection board.

Many aviators rolling ashore want duty in the fleet replacement squadrons, weapons schools, or test pilot school. Very few seek nonflying orders such as Washington (Pentagon) duty or assignment to NPS for a master's degree. They want "hours in type" (that is, flight hours in their specific type/model/series of aircraft) to be more competitive for command screen boards when their time comes. Most officers in all warfare communities understandably want to stay close to their profession. It is where they can stay in touch and be evaluated by rising seniors, rather than getting lost in the academic world and being out of sight and out of mind for as long as two to four years. The outcome of these concerns leads many officers to pick up a degree while on shore duty (for example, the Naval Academy's company officer degree program and the Naval War College degree program).

While a limited number of ensigns are selected for immediate graduate programs, most officers finish the commissioning pipeline and, after the sea duty pipeline, head to their first assignment for warfare qualification and the first sea tour. At some point in the next few years, you will be eligible for a shore tour, and you should consider assignment to a postgraduate education course at NPS or a civilian university offering a degree in a service-relatable field. Your input and requests to the talent management boards are your entry to the process for shore duty assignment and the opportunity for graduate school.[4] Your engagement with the community mentors, your family, and your early communication with detailers will provide the best insight to these opportunities and reflection on the benefit of graduate education to your future career.

The Navy expects to invest in its future leaders as critical/strategic thinkers. The point of these observations is to encourage you to seriously consider seeking a two- to three-year postgraduate course. Some risks are involved that might be overlooked in the rush to get a degree or to return from sea to what is perceived as a less demanding professional environment ashore. The risks include future assignment to a specialty only tenuously related to the postgraduate course attended, being away from your warfare specialty for too long, and having little time left for a professional military education program essential to your further career progress. It comes down to how you and your detailer work to use your scarce time and how much you like the hard work in the classroom.

Professional Military Education

Attendance at a war college will improve your professional performance in that you will get a wider perspective of the naval profession and national security. It may not necessarily make you a better commanding officer of a fleet unit, but it will improve your performance as a staff officer in Washington and elsewhere and give you some of the intellectual underpinnings needed for high command. PME is designed to prepare all service officers to operate in joint military operations, with an understanding of joint planning, doctrine, and command and control for current and future wartime contingencies.

After a long holiday (roughly 1945 to 1990) in which attendance at one of the many war and staff colleges was not essential to career progression, PME programs have returned to their previous importance. In the current Department of Defense policy, "All officers should make a continuing, strong personal commitment to their professional development beyond the formal schooling offered in the military educational system. Officers share responsibility for ensuring continued growth of themselves and others."[5] Completion of PME courses is expected at all levels of officership, and completion of the PME curriculum is now essential for consideration for promotion to flag rank. But there are many ways to fill this requirement. There are long and short courses, and there are courses at the institutions of the other services. Moreover, there are qualifying correspondence courses for those who are particularly pressed for time and cannot squeeze in a residential course.

Although it is not anti-intellectual anymore, the naval service is faced with the realities of competing priorities that tend to push higher education aside. Those competing priorities are an emphasis on youthful service leadership, extended sea duty pipeline training, obligatory tour(s) in Washington and in joint duty, and the historical practice of highly valuing tours at sea (the longer, the better).

Issues in Making a Decision

Submitting a future duty preference card to the community talent management board for a tour in postgraduate education or at a war college requires your careful consideration. The issues include: Should you do it and, if so, when in your career? Do you have time in your career path? In what area or areas of study are you interested, and will they have application to your future positions? Do you stay in the school of hard knocks, or do you broaden your educational base and enhance your résumé? If school is an option, which school and major should be selected? Navy career development, family environment and impact, and post-Navy options are all part of the conversation.

One theory of career progression is that at most, you have only one "throwaway tour" in a career. Your detailers will not like that phrase; to them, every billet is important because they must fill it. In their view, the assignment they have in mind will likely be intended to improve your future military marketability. Because more career "wickets" are involved, submariners and aviators may have less latitude in making such offline choices. With all the other previously stated considerations, assignment to a postgraduate program might still be the right answer. Many have reflected on the tour at NPS as a time to decompress and refocus on family and career aspirations. The curriculum is still rigorous, but the balance of work and family life seems easier to manage in the collegial atmosphere of Monterey, California. An additional reminder is that completing the graduate degree comes with additional obligated service, so it is by no means a free pass out of the Navy to a civilian career.

This last comment requires additional reflection. In the past there has been a high demand from junior officers to be at or near a school where they could obtain a master of business administration (MBA) degree. Their prevailing opinion is that this degree is the ticket to a better career opportunity outside the Navy. Senior Navy leadership has agreed with this perception and, therefore, has removed the MBA from the NPS catalog and is moving more toward degrees in Department of Defense management, which are more aligned to PME and joint requirements.

Having been in the acquisition professional side of our Navy and worked for many years in the civilian side of our defense industry, I see differing sides to this debate. First is that the principles learned in the MBA curriculum have very helpful and practical application in any Navy leadership position. Learning the fundamental in economics, management, organizational theory, communications, and leadership can only help officers be more effective in their critical leadership positions. Second, as a hiring manager in the defense industry, the MBA is not the guarantee of being hired or assurance of a higher starting salary. The totality of the résumé and demonstrated past performance (going back to chapter 1) is the key to achieving the position and pay. As far as the Navy is concerned, attrition is not determined by the promises of an MBA; rather, retention is the result of an officer's reflection on past assignments and the commanding officers who demonstrate good leadership and a commitment to the mission of the Navy.

Do It Yourself

Another option is to get advanced education on your own. Extension courses at a local university, war college correspondence courses, and other individual study opportunities are readily available. A major factor in your school program should be self-study. You do not have to go to school to learn. Nor do you need to rely solely on experience to prepare yourself for what you will face downstream in a naval career. Much of your education is in your own capable hands (and is supported utilizing your GI Bill education benefits).

In pursuit of a degree or not, hopefully you will always be in the pursuit of learning. While President of the Naval War College Vice Adm. James Stockdale emphasized the important trait of continual self-improvement.⁶ Professionally and personally, we should seek to be better morally, mentally, and physically. And the Naval War College and other service colleges continuously improve the access to and variety of their libraries and online curriculum. Thanks to the U.S. Naval Institute and other military publishers, some excellent books are available for reminding you of our remarkable Navy history and instructing you in your duties and in your approach to your profession. Additionally, I also recommend the different and changing reading lists out there from the CNO, MCPON (Master Chief Petty Officer of the Navy), and the other service chiefs. If you are assigned to the Pentagon, you will have access to the Pentagon library—use it! We all have access to the Defense Department Morale, Welfare, and Recreation libraries. Last, have a local library card, and have your own catalog of favorite historical and inspirational books on your phone or tablet device.

Many have chosen this do-it-yourself route to obtain their degree; however, be aware that the Navy's renewed attention to graduate education sees in-residence education programs as the best opportunity to mature critical/strategic thinking skills. And going forward, the major command graduate requirement will not be met through distance learning education.

Our Navy needs you to have a "liberal education" including the technical expertise in the mechanics to arm, train, maintain, and fight.⁷ While you learn how to learn in the undergraduate programs, the postgraduate opportunities should build on your education base to better prepare you for the rigors of operational duty, making you more competent, confident, and marketable for future demanding assignments. You may find yourself overwhelmed with studying papers or official documents that are in your inbox. Nonetheless, carefully consider the opportunity for orders to graduate school, and prioritize regular access to educational and informational material that will make you better prepared to address local political and environmental concerns and be more able to lead in the time of crisis.

At the Naval Academy we say that the purpose of training is to deal with the known and expected; education prepares us to deal with the unknown and unexpected.

9

SEA/SHORE ROTATION AND HOMESTEADING

Home is where the Navy sends us.
—Popular Navy wall placard

The orders you will receive for assignment to a new duty station are called PCS (permanent change of station) orders. The ironic point is that there is nothing permanent about those orders. The entire Navy assignment system is built around rotation from sea duty to shore duty and back, and PCS duty assignments might be as short as a year and rarely longer than three years. This fact is driven by both the arithmetic of the numbers of sea and shore billets and the need to have proficient officers at sea and seasoned officers in shore billets. A side benefit is to give officers a chance to broaden their career skills ashore. Following in importance is the desire to give officers a respite from the constant deployments and family separations inherent in most sea duty. Management of your sea/shore rotation is a necessity for your professional development. Long extensions on sea duty might be professionally gratifying and fun, and long extensions on shore duty may give you more time with your family, but either can throw your career progression off pace. If you extend on sea duty or overseas shore duty, it probably means that you are going from a ship or squadron to a staff or fleet support activity that is technically sea duty. If you extend (or are extended) ashore, it means you are being delayed in getting important sea qualifications.

My advice is to accept rotation as an immutable pattern of life and plan accordingly. When junior, the balance is tipped in favor of sea duty (again, the proportion of junior billets at sea and ashore drives this), and as you get more senior, you will find that shore tours are longer and that sea tours become shorter. Fast-track aviator captains are an exception; often they will spend almost all their time in grade at sea. Nevertheless, by the time you are a captain and have twenty-four to twenty-five years of service, most of you can plan to spend the rest of your time ashore. Plenty of jobs—most of them good—are available, even if a flag is not in your future.

The temptation also exists to extend your tour at sea. After all, that is where the real action is. But one of the objectives in your career planning is balance. The possibility is real that the upcoming Washington tour will do more for your professional growth than an additional tour at sea—particularly if you go to a sea staff. If an extension at sea or shore means an early or additional command tour, by all means, take it. But bonus commands are rare in these days of a smaller Navy.

Homesteading

You will hear the term "homesteading" often. The good news is that the term no longer carries a pejorative connotation. For a time, the homesteader title was pinned on a service member who was not career-minded and chose current location over the harder job and the need to relocate. But today, it simply means that you get two or more back-to-back tours in different commands at the same location. You might go from sea to shore in the same city, such as

Norfolk, San Diego, or Pearl Harbor—that is, wherever there is a concentration of naval activity. And you can accomplish this while taking the next hard job and staying competitive with your community group.

There is a trend toward homesteading in the Navy. Wardrooms filled with young, single, and highly mobile officers are gone. In their place, we find young married officers, married officers with many years of prior enlisted service, and officers married to other service members. We find officers with spouses who have demanding, rewarding jobs; we find officers who have older children—children who are more settled and more involved in high school or community activities and less interested in moving every two years. More than before, families are investing in homes rather than accepting military housing. This financial commitment and the volatile housing market drive roots deeper and make moving harder. For these reasons, "ship type" has been bumped by "home port" as the number-one priority on surface warfare officer preference cards.[1]

But the caution is presented here because the opportunity for two (or more) career-enhancing tours back to back in the same locality may not be as available as you wish. The more frequent homesteading case is to "roll" from a good sea job to a lesser shore job. Ambitious officers cannot afford to spend any or much time in lesser jobs; in accepting them, they incur the risk of future disappointment in the screening and assignment processes.

Exceptions exist, however. For example, you might roll out of your good sea billet in a unit homeported in Norfolk and be ordered to the Joint Forces Staff College, thereby buffing up your joint credentials. Or as a squadron skipper at Oceana, you may be ordered to command a fleet replacement squadron (as a bonus). Or you may be ordered to a good job on the staff of a real up-and-comer and have an opportunity to show what you can do before an appreciative potential mentor. But the exceptions need to be considered carefully. Sad but true: the odds are high that another tour in the same locality will not be the best career move.

Detailers in many cases like homesteading because it saves them money out of their travel budget (which is always pressed), and often they can get you to your new duty station quicker (which is important if the billet is gapped or the officer you are relieving is needed somewhere else quickly). But your best interests are not always served by making it easy for detailers. Although they want to make you happy and more promotable, they also have a job to do—billets to fill quickly, travel funds to save, and so on. And they can always make a persuasive case for accepting the billet under consideration.

As often reiterated in this text, regular communication with your family, mentors, and detailer is a must to make your desires known and give the system the chance of meeting your goals. As a senior detailer, I drew out and presented the officers' potential career path. This records their previous duty and qualifications and lays out the "best" plan for achieving their command opportunity and promotion to O-6. What was always added were the years when their children were going to be in high school. This extenuating and important factor was often a driver to consider where the next best opportunity might be. This also has driven many to consider the option of being a geographic bachelor. The benefits of stability of schools and friends need to be weighed against the cost of two residences, regular travel, and the "deployment mode" while on shore duty. Getting the right balance of the detailer's triad—needs of the Navy, your career, and your personal desires—is a difficult process and requires your careful consideration.

A regular point of conversation among career military families are declarations of how many moves the family made and how many different schools their children attended. Hanging below the

"Home" wall placard are the addresses of the many duty stations where the family has resided. Whether the memories are positive or not so great, these are reminders of the demands of a military career. If you are offered an opportunity to homestead where you are, find out what other transfer opportunities are available, opportunities that may entail a personal (family) hardship but are more career-enhancing. Good deals are rare in the promotion sweepstakes. The easier the job and the more congenial the situation, the less attractive the job is likely to be in the promotion context.

Overseas Tours

You will find a greater proportion of overseas billets than there used to be, and they are in more challenging locales. While the lure of an exciting or exotic location is attractive, the overseas billets are basically "forward-deployed" and are the first line of defense in the theaters of concern. So, there is a high operational tempo, and the "tourist" promotion of overseas (or outside the continental United States, including Hawai'i, Alaska, and U.S. territories) home ports is often overstated. In each of the recent years on ship selection night for the Naval Academy graduating surface warfare officers, the very first ships to be picked are homeported in Rota, Spain. The next most popular duty stations are in Japan and Hawai'i. The attraction of being far away and in new and exciting locations is clear. The follow-up, however, is that the duty at such sites can be much more rigorous and taxing than being homeported in Norfolk, Virginia. Underway periods are more frequent and often on short notice. There are heightened security issues requiring smaller number of duty sections, and the ability to travel can be regularly restricted.[2] (In 2022 the U.S. Navy announced the reopening of Naval Base Subic Bay in the Philippines. Not used as a naval port since 1992, the change in policy has raised the opportunity for additional U.S. Navy presence in the South China Sea.[3])

Yet, the odds are high that you may be ordered overseas at some point in your career. Today's detailers and their bosses recognize the challenges associated with overseas tours and look favorably on the records of officers who have accepted the assignment, especially those who agree to overseas *sea* duty, not necessarily spending three to four years in London. If you have the desire, or if the detailers are batting your name around for an overseas assignment, the best advice is to contact a peer who is in that location now, for the best reflection on the pluses and minuses of such an assignment. Then, look forward to your rotation orders as another opportunity to broaden your career background.

The United States Naval Academy welcomes the incoming fourth-class midshipmen, or plebes, of the class of 2027. Induction day (I-day) marks the beginning of a demanding six-week indoctrination period called plebe summer, intended to transition the candidates from civilian to military life. Taking the oath of office on this first day starts their Navy career journey. *Photo by Stacy Godfrey*

A Marine Corps drill instructor assigned to Officer Training Command Newport, Rhode Island, congratulates officer candidate school (OCS) students during the battle stations completion ceremony. OCS is the commissioning route for graduates from a traditional four-year college, enlisted members transitioning into officer roles, or direct commission officers with specialized skills or professional degrees. *Photo by Darwin Lam*

Then-CNO Adm. Lisa Franchetti administers the oath of office during the George Washington University NROTC commissioning ceremony in spring 2024. The largest single source of Navy and Marine Corps officers, the NROTC scholarship program plays an important role in preparing young men and women for leadership positions in the naval service. *Photo by Chief Petty Officer Amanda Gray*

Officers from the Japan Maritime Self-Defense Force present a ceremonial samurai sword to the first midshipman to select a ship out of Sasebo, Japan, during the annual ship selection night at the U.S. Naval Academy. For surface warfare officers, the first ship selection is a key event in the officer's professional journey, and overseas billets are highly desirable. Approximately 250 midshipmen, who will serve as surface warfare officers upon graduation and commissioning, participate in the event. *Photo by Kenneth D. Aston*

U.S. Naval Academy midshipmen of the Class of 2021 respond to the oath of office with "I do!" during their graduation and commissioning ceremony. "I will well and faithfully discharge the duties of the office upon which I am about to enter" is a reminder that sustained superior performance is an obligation, not an option. *Photo by Mass Communication Specialist 2nd Class Dana D. Legg*

Early qualification in an officer's warfare area is the right start to a successful Navy career. Having technical competence is a must, and seeking mentoring and coaching along the way will keep you on a career track. Here, the carrier air wing operations officer checks in on the first flight in an F/A-18F Super Hornet attached to the "Diamondbacks" of Strike Fighter Squadron (VFA) 102, on the flight deck of the USS *Ronald Reagan* (CVN 76). *Photo by Mass Communication Specialist 3rd Class Gray Gibson*

The surface warfare community is the fastest track to fleet assignments and Navy leadership positions. Standing bridge watch on the *San Antonio*–class amphibious transport dock ship USS *Arlington* (LPD 24), this ensign provides pelorus training for a midshipman on a summer cruise. *Photo by Mass Communication Specialist 2nd Class John Bellino*

The *Virginia*-class fast-attack submarine USS *Vermont* (SSN 792), the first Block IV *Virginia*-class submarine to enter service, arrives at its new home port of Joint Base Pearl Harbor–Hickam. The MK1, MOD0 submarine career path is tightly managed to ensure junior officers complete initial training and are submarine- and engineer-qualified, staying on track for the important department head assignment. *Photo by Mass Communication Specialist 1st Class Chris Williamson*

A surface warfare ensign greets his Navy officer spouse on the pier after returning from patrol aboard the *Arleigh Burke*–class guided-missile destroyer USS *Roosevelt* (DDG 80), homeported in Rota, Spain. *Roosevelt* completed her fourth patrol in the U.S. Naval Forces Europe area of operations, employed by U.S. 6th Fleet to defend U.S., allied, and partner interests. *Photo by Petty Officer 2nd Class Danielle Baker*

Navy career planning may include the consideration of a lateral transfer to another warfare community. Engineering duty officers (EDOs) lean on their warfare qualification and advanced technical degrees to oversee ship/submarine construction and maintenance. Here, the EDO docking officer directs as the USS *North Carolina* (SSN 777) is being drydocked for her depot modernization period at Pearl Harbor Naval Shipyard. *Photo by Justice Vannatta*

The *Arleigh Burke*–class guided-missile destroyer USS *McFaul* (DDG 74) returns to home port at Naval Station Norfolk, Virginia, after an eight-month deployment to the U.S. 6th Fleet area of operations. Sea-shore rotation is the framework of the naval service. The operating cycle and deployments will continue to be driven by world events and the need for the worldwide presence of the U.S. Navy. *Photo by Petty Officer 1st Class Ryan Seelbach*

After an initial sea tour, a junior officer has a lot to consider for a first shore tour—to meet personal goals while not getting far from the community career track. Postgraduate school is very desirable, but the detailer may be suggesting more time in the schoolhouse or production assignment. Here, in the shore duty assignment of a fleet replacement squadron (FRS), two pilots from Patrol Squadron (VP) 30 fly a P-8A Poseidon maritime patrol aircraft during a scheduled training flight. *Photo by Petty Officer 1st Class Curtis Spencer*

Crews for precommissioning units have a unique opportunity and challenge. Being a plank owner is a special recognition, but during the construction phase, commands need to be creative with cross-rate and cross-deck training to ensure the crew maintains operational proficiency. Here, the crew of the *Virginia*-class attack submarine precommissioning unit *Idaho* (SSN 799) marches during a christening ceremony in Groton, Connecticut. *Photo by John Narewski*

Ship and aviation squadron leadership assignments often include the left seat–right seat policy, where orders for the executive officer include the assignment to fleet up to the commanding officer position. Here, the executive officer of the guided-missile destroyer USS *Sterett* (DDG 104) discusses plans with officers on the bridge as the ship gets underway from Naval Base San Diego for surface warfare advanced tactical training. *Photo by Mass Communication Specialist 1st Class Daniel Barker*

The deputy chief of naval operations for operations, plans, and strategy hosts his Japanese counterpart from the Japan Maritime Self-Defense Force at the Pentagon. Tours in the Pentagon provide a unique opportunity to see (how the Navy runs) and be seen (by serving with the highest Navy and other service officials). This important shore duty assignment might be a big step in one's career and could present significant work-life balance challenges that should be carefully considered. *Photo by Petty Officer 2nd Class Jonteil Johnson*

A tour at the Naval War College (NWC) is a valuable experience for a joint education and completion of joint professional military education. A tour at Navy Personnel Command (NPC) gives one insight into the Navy's complex personnel management system. Here, the president of NWC briefs detailers, officer community managers, and junior officers from the Bureau of Naval Personnel assigned to NPC about the NWC mission, its value to the fleet, and why an NWC education is important to an officer's career. *Photo by Daniel S. Marciniak*

From junior to senior ranks, a Navy officer must be comfortable and proficient at briefing. The commander of U.S. 7th Fleet addresses junior officers assigned to surface forces during the surface warfare summit hosted by Destroyer Squadron 15. The 7th Fleet is the U.S. Navy's largest forward-deployed numbered fleet and routinely interacts and operates with allies and partners in preserving a free and open Indo-Pacific region. *Photo by Petty Officer 2nd Class Caitlin Flynn*

The commanding officer of the amphibious assault carrier USS *Tripoli* (LHA 7) administers the oath of office during a promotion ceremony. The effective Navy leader is committed to the development and promotion of their Sailors. The importance of meaningful, well-written evaluations and timely recognition with awards cannot be overstated. *Photo by Mass Communication Specialist 3rd Class Maci Sternod*

Being greeted in Dili, Timor-Leste, as part of the Cooperation Afloat Readiness and Training, the commanding officer of USS *John P. Murtha* (LPD 26) receives some local uniform accoutrements. The worldwide presence of the Navy provides many unique opportunities and requires the awareness and acceptance of local customs to represent our Navy well. *Photo by Petty Officer 2nd Class Joshua Samoluk*

Sustained superior performance leads to achieving one's goals of promotion and command. The offgoing commanding officer, Surface Warfare Schools Command, passes through sideboys at the end of the change of command ceremony at Naval Station Newport. Command at sea and major command ashore are positions to be cherished. *Photo by Petty Officer 2nd Class Derien Luce*

The "Merlins" of Helicopter Sea Combat Wing Pacific host the retirement ceremony for the commander. A change of command and retirement ceremony is the opportunity to pull out all the stops—for the Navy to acknowledge the long and faithful career of the retiring officer. It is also the chance for officers to reflect on their careers and acknowledge the impact and importance of mentors, coaches, shipmates, and family. *Photo by Petty Officer 2nd Class Sara Eshleman*

The "golden anchor" is a large and bold symbol recognizing the Retention Excellence Award for sustaining superior levels of military retention. Proud Sailors paint the starboard anchor aboard the aircraft carrier USS *John C. Stennis* (CVN 74) in Bremerton, Washington. *Photo by Navy Petty Officer 3rd Class Dakota Rayburn*

10

COMMAND AND STAFF ASSIGNMENTS

> When you are in command, command.
> —Adm. Chester Nimitz

> In the absence of any other orders, always march to the sound of the guns.
> —Napoleon

Hopefully, any officer reading this text would see their compass needle pointing to command and find the instructions and suggestions here helpful for reaching that pinnacle of service. For those in the Navy unrestricted line, they want to become COs of ships, subs, aviation squadrons, or seagoing special warfare units. Those who aspire to promotion in the supply corps, civil engineering corps, or the various other staff and restricted-line specialties may still find this chapter helpful as they will have shore command opportunities and may be working for the unrestricted line at points in their own career journey.

Command and preparing yourself for it are the name of the game. Only the rare bird in the unrestricted line makes captain in the Navy without having had a command tour, preferably at sea, and preferably a successful one. Almost all have to achieve command in the grade of commander to stay in the professional performance and promotion success business. Within the surface warfare officer community, there are early command opportunities on minesweepers (MCMs) or naval support elements commanding landing craft, the likes of landing craft air cushion, landing craft utility (LCUs), and lighter, amphibious resupply, cargo vehicles (LARCs). Additionally, and as addressed before, changes in technology and strategy create new opportunities. Lieutenant commander and lieutenant commands will soon be available for light amphibious warships (LAWs) and the unmanned task group automated unmanned systems (UxS).[1]

Although all services place great emphasis on command experience, for the naval officer it is the only game in town. No officers are considered proven until they have served in command. No responsibility is so absolute as command at sea. All the good staff jobs in the world, no matter how ably performed, cannot rescue a résumé that does not have a successful command tour. The Navy ethos places shore duty and staff duty much further down the line in importance. They are necessary but not central to the Navy's mission. Somebody must perform those duties, and there are benefits—for example, improving your understanding of the Navy as a whole, broadening your service reputation among other warfare specialties, and providing an opportunity for more home life. A Navy mentor will tell you, "Go to sea, young man and woman, and prepare yourself for command." And your mentor and detailer should be working with you to ensure you remain competitive for the command position and that you are competent and confident in assuming this grand responsibility.

Why is there this seemingly myopic focus on sea duty and command? It is what the Navy is all about, where the forces are, where the action is, and where the challenges of battle with the enemy are faced and met. It is where you put your career on the line every day. It is where Sailors are an integral part of your life and a leadership challenge. This saliency of command is a fact of life of the sea service and always has been. Its roots go back to the early days of the Navy when the shore establishment was nearly nonexistent. If you were a naval officer, you were at sea, or you were ashore on half pay. By definition, a naval officer was a sea officer.

In the 1980s we had a strategic plan for a six-hundred-ship Navy. Over time and for various reasons, that numerical goal was never achieved. With the advent of new technologies and new classes of ships, the current inventory of commissioned Navy ships and submarines lies just under 280. The current ship-building plan is to reach 373 ships and subs by 2045.[2] For your career, it is important to consider and be attentive to the changes in the force and how one might stay relevant and competitive for new opportunities. By the time you complete a thirty-year career, you will be able to list ships you served on that have long been decommissioned. Be flexible, stay relevant, and be available to take command.

Of course, the institution and infrastructure of the Navy also changed, and we now have a massive shore establishment to support a highly complex and technical Navy. And there are many important command billets ashore—in the training establishment, recruiting offices, fleet support activities, and industrial support base of the service. But nothing beats the visibility, prestige, and professional growth opportunity of a sea command billet.

In the 1943 first edition of the Naval Institute Press publication *Command at Sea*, author Capt. Harley F. Cole, USN, spoke of command in this way:

> Every young officer who is worth his salt looks forward eagerly to his first command, whether it be a destroyer, minesweeper, a submarine, a PT, or an auxiliary. There is a tremendous thrill in taking over your first ship. She is your ship—all yours—but the way to

success is dotted with pitfalls for the unwary, the careless, and the diffident. From the moment you, as the new skipper, step aboard, you are on trial before your officers and men. Responsibility for the ship as well as the crew is yours.

Particularly in time of war, when promotion is rapid and officers with comparatively little experience must frequently assume command, it is important that the officer has complete an understanding as possible of the special duties and tasks with which he will be faced—the duties of both the task force and the independent naval operations, and the responsibility of maintaining a happy and efficient ship.

The officer with many years of sea experience has been afforded the opportunity to observe various commanding officers. Perhaps unconsciously he has thought to himself, "If I were skipper I would do it this way," and when command comes to him he has already made definite plans regarding the course he intends to follow. The inexperienced junior officer getting his first command often wishes that such opportunities had been afforded him.

There is no formula for success as a commanding officer. Some officers are natural leaders, others not. Some have the benefit of a long and good background of experience under competent commanding officers that others have not enjoyed. Some make mistakes, but it must be remembered that mistakes are greatly magnified if committed a second or third time, for one is expected to profit from mistakes.[3]

I have included this long introduction from the 1943 edition of *Command at Sea* because after six editions of the text, the U.S. Naval Institute authors have continued to introduce the book with Captain Cole's time-honored reflection on command. Any additions can only address inclusion of the qualification of women in command, and the consideration of the various other Navy commands. On a ship, everything inside the lifelines is your responsibility. In a squadron, everything on the flight line and in the hangars is yours. On a base, everything inside the gate and fences belongs to you. The responsibility of the commanding officer is absolute, and he or she is to "exercise leadership through personal example, moral responsibility, and judicious attention to the welfare of the persons under their supervision."[4] This is what everyone expects, and Navy regulations require.

If a successful command tour and multiple preparatory sea tours are so important, two questions arise. What is the pathway to command? How do officers prepare themselves for such a race? Every journey starts with the first step, and the path to command starts very early in one's career. Although initial missteps can be overcome, it becomes more difficult to correct for wrong turns or less than excellent performance as tour builds on tour. View your career as building a brick wall, laying one brick on another. Strong foundations lead to expanded career opportunities.

As Captain Cole points out, there are significant benefits to observing your present CO and, as stated before, benefits to mentally fleeting up to consider what lessons are to be learned from the individual or situation. *Command at Sea* provides great insight, checklists, and examples of the myriad duties and responsibilities that might be encountered in command. This is helpful forethought for when your command confronts new and unexpected situations. Once in the designated pipeline for command, the Naval Leadership and Ethics Center in Newport, Rhode Island, is in the forefront to prepare the command triad (CO, XO, Command Master Chief/ Chief of the Boat) for success. An additional consideration is the book *Destroyer Captain: Lessons of a First Command*, by Adm. James Stavridis, USN (Ret.).[5] The text is a reduction of daily journals he kept during his command tour aboard the USS *Barry* (DDG-52). The importance of this text is that it encompasses more than one campaign, deployment, or battle. The admiral brings to your attention the highs and lows, the expectations and pressures, the exciting and the mundane, the pride and disappointments of being in command.

Hopefully, command is in your sights. There are great models and mentors to help show you the way and to reflect on previous directions in this text, to do your utmost to perform well in the job you have today, to make your command and skipper successful, and to prepare yourself meticulously for your boss's job.

Staff duty is not command, but these important assignments get you as close to the commanders as possible. These positions will broaden your professional perspective and expose you to the notice and leadership of some of the Navy's top people. But staff duty cannot be the strength of your résumé if you aspire to command. In the other services, you might make a career of staff duty, but not so in the Navy. Staffs are a way station, not a destination for the ambitious naval officer. With regard to staff duty, staffs are necessary as long as we have large organizations. Admirals are necessary at sea as long as naval forces include many (often differing) units that must act in concert. Staffs help the admirals plan, decide, and supervise. Staff officers are not in charge of things outside the confines of the staff. Their role is to gather information, plan, advise, and monitor. They do not act for the admiral except in areas where the admiral's policy and intent are very clear. They are not in command. And they do not bear ultimate responsibility for the performance of the units under their admiral's command. Your goal, however, regardless of the staff role, should be as previously suggested—do your utmost to perform well in the job you have today, to make your staff and your boss successful. You may not aspire to the staff position, but you can learn so much from the Navy staff operations.

Command and Staff Assignments

As an option, then, consider staff duties an adjunct to your career, but not the main route. The biggest exception is, of course, duty on a staff in Washington. Almost all Washington duty is staff duty, but there it is staff duty of a special kind. The closer to the top you are, the closer you are to determining (or seeing determined) the future of your service. The further away from the top you are (for example, a destroyer squadron staff or an air wing commander's staff), the more you see how today's Navy operates. But if you are alert, you can learn about today's operations in your ship and squadron tours and move on to having your staff duty in Washington, where, to a large degree, the Navy's and your future will be determined.

In a chapter titled "Command," I feel it is appropriate to present a vignette that I have repeated to "leaders" on every rung of the chain of command.

We talk about command as if it is a singular position that is recognized by the gold star (command at sea insignia) or the gold trident (command ashore insignia). And when authorized to wear the pin above the right pocket (while in command; over the left pocket, post-command), we have this expectation that Admiral Nimitz's aphorism applies to you: when in command, command.

My mentor would regularly recite Nimitz as a way to encourage me to boldly accept more responsibility and make hard, well-thought-out decisions. The point was, command is not limited to those wearing the command insignia.[6] Whenever there is anyone looking to you for advice, direction, correction, or encouragement, you are in command. So, command!

The application to this philosophy extends from the 4/C midshipman to the four-star admiral, from the E-1 to the E-9. There are always times that we are in a position to positively influence the attitude and performance of others. Make the most of each experience, and make command a state of mind and not a position.

11

WASHINGTON DUTY

> Into most successful careers, a little Washington must fall.
> —Adm. James Stavridis

As a junior officer, you are not yet thinking about Washington duty. And from what you may have heard, you don't want to think about Washington duty. It is more likely that your first shore duty will be in one of your community's schoolhouses. But by your second shore tour, the odds of your going to Washington duty are very high. To come ashore from a challenging sea billet to an office in the Washington bureaucracy where the office's product is not at all apparent—or, if apparent, seemingly unimportant—can be a real letdown. Yet, if you are not at sea, your career is usually best served by duty in Washington (or headquarters that are an extension of Washington, such as the Navy Personnel Command in Millington, Tennessee, or the Naval Air Systems Command at Patuxent River, Maryland).

To be clear, when we talk of Washington duty, the reference is concerning your assignment to the Pentagon. Having a cubicle somewhere within the six million square feet of office space, shared with some thirty thousand military and civilian employees who support all the services, will be new. Your office is labeled by floor (B through 4), ring (A through E), corridor (1–10), and room (1–99).

Washington Duty

Asking for directions is quite acceptable and routine. To highlight the complexity that one confronts in an initial tour in the Pentagon, Rear Adm. Fred Kacher, in the *Naval Officer's Guide to the Pentagon*, opens the book with fourteen pages listing "some" of the programmatic acronyms and abbreviations you would want to be familiar with.[1]

The more senior you get, the more time you will and should spend in Washington, because that is where the major decisions that employ today's Navy and create tomorrow's Navy are made. If you are interested in a top Navy job someday, you have to understand how those decisions are made and in your own modest way contribute to them. It may not be fun, the hours are often long, the decision matrix is cumbersome, and your commute may be frustrating; however, when we talk about the good hard jobs, many reside in the Washington headquarters. This section is not meant to recruit for or dissuade you from seeking a Washington position, but hopefully you will gain some insight that will make a tour in the Pentagon an option.

A few flag officers take pride in the fact that they never had Washington duty. For the most part, they belong to a different era, or they will have a difficult time getting in the running for the Navy's top jobs. Unfortunately, being a "good operator" is not enough. You also need to be a good force acquisition, management, planning, or budgeting person or some combination of these, and you learn that in Washington. One of the more concerning sights in Washington is to run into flag officers who are on their first Washington assignment. They are learning in a hurry and are probably too late. They pine to get back to sea, but they will likely never again get there while on active duty. What does Washington duty do for your career and promotion prospects?

Washington: Where the Top Jobs Are

Most of the Navy's flag (and even captain) jobs are in the Washington area or associated headquarters. If you aspire to high rank, you may spend most of your time ashore as a senior officer in Washington. Washington tours are also the precondition for getting the top jobs in the fleet. How does this work?

By the time you are a senior commander or captain, you may have had, or are in, your second or subsequent Washington tour. You are learning how the Navy plans for its future, budgets and programs to survive in the funding world, prospers in the joint world, and supports the operations of the fleet at the major headquarters level. You are learning the trade of getting things done in the nation's capital. It is rather like watching sausage being made. It is not pretty, but unfortunately it is necessary. These preparatory tours are important for your career. You should be looking ahead to the day when your promotion jacket is before the flag selection board and its members are asking each other the following: what can this officer do to help us carry the Navy's load at headquarters as well as at sea? They ask this question because your first billet after you are selected for flag rank probably will be in Washington. As a junior flag officer in Washington, you will be doing important Navy business—and looking forward to getting to a flag job afloat. You will not get that afloat job if you do not perform well in Washington, and getting up on step in Washington as a boot flag officer is much easier if you know the lay of the land.

Getting Known

In the original edition of this book, Rear Admiral Winnefeld reflected about a friend—a war hero and senior officer unfortunately not destined to make flag. The personal conclusion was, "The biggest mistake I made in my career was not to get known." What this officer realized (too late) was that although he had a good record—and in combat, at that—he never looked for assignments that broadened his résumé. He had only one brief Washington tour and was always in a hurry to get back to the fleet. His desire was understandable, except that it did little to expand the basis for his service reputation beyond his warfare community.

For most, Washington tours are our first extended and close-up experience interacting with officers in other warfare specialties and other services. If you are a ship driver, you have had little opportunity for such interaction with aviators and submariners. And the same applies to officers who serve in those specialties. In Washington, the odds are high that you will be working for an officer in another warfare specialty and that your daily business will be conducted with officers outside your warfare community. This is an important opportunity to display your professional competence before a larger audience. Although your future screening boards will be comprised of seniors from your warfare community, they will be in a minority in your future promotion boards. (For the restricted line officers, it may be helpful to have your FITREPs reviewed by an unrestricted line officer, as they will comprise the majority of your boards.)

Over the years, many senior officers have come to the conclusion that it is often officers from other communities whose vote pushes you over the top into the next promotion. It is not enough for your community to be high on you; your record must persuade others, too. The spadework to get their vote usually starts with your Washington assignments with a set of fitness reports signed by bosses outside your warfare specialty but well known by board members from those communities. The greatest benefit of Washington duty (as with other staff positions) is you get to know and be known. Both aspects should be important to you. See how decisions are made so you will be better prepared to make them yourself, and be seen as a top performer who should at any later date be given the opportunity to be that decision-maker.

Networking

It is the rare officer on duty in Washington who does not have to work with departments and commands outside their own. Much of the work in Washington involves working with other offices. This need results in a great deal of networking to get the Navy's business done. A by-product is that you get known outside of your own office and get a reputation as a doer or a roadblock, a person who works the problem or one who bucks it up to the boss, someone who is a team player or a loner. There is another important by-product, too: when you get back to the fleet, you will know how Washington works. You will not be intimidated by the bureaucracy (you were once part of it), and you will not hesitate for long to call a contact in Washington to get the answers or support you need.

A Word About Washington Working Hours

Some of you may be looking forward to your Washington tour, thinking you may have an opportunity to spend more time with your family after back-to-back arduous overseas deployments. Talk to someone stationed there now! Unfortunately, the more regular and more predictable your working hours in Washington, the further away you are from the real action. Working hours should be not be your objective. True, some offices work long hours because that is the boss's style, and some even enjoy it for the bragging rights it brings. But in most offices, long working hours mean that things are happening or about to happen and that the organization is responding or trying to get out ahead of the problem. A phone call from a congressional staffer on needed funding or a bill before the committee stimulates the system; so does that late phone call (inevitably on a Friday afternoon when you are cleaning out your inbox) from an official in the office of the secretary of defense or from a four-star fleet commander. Your chain of command may be so busy putting out fires during regular working hours that they find that the routine work must be done after most other offices are closing down.

The point of this discussion is that when you hear an office in the Pentagon has routine working hours that run from eight in the morning to five in the afternoon, be wary and skeptical about that assignment. Chances are that they are not close to the heartbeat of the action or that the product of that shop is routine staffing. As a corollary, look carefully at the shop that is working long hours so you can satisfy yourself that their work is really all that important and that their bosses carry a lot of weight in the larger scheme of things.

The work schedule in the Pentagon can be difficult, exacerbated by a long and busy commute. While some offices have been experimenting with some remote work hours (lessons from post–COVID-19 experiences), most offices are required to do the work in the "building." It is shore duty, and it is where the heartbeat of our Navy is driven. So the balance of important work and life is a challenge that some do not manage well. I was aware of one flag officer who had two executive assistants (on shift work). The flag officer "lived" at the Pentagon and was not willing to make his staff work his hours. Another of my bosses would say, "If you have nothing to do, don't do it here!"—meaning that if you have your work done, go home. There were a few rare occasions where that was accomplished!

Follow the Dollars

The power in Washington resides closest to the dollars—that is, getting them from Congress and spending them on the things the Navy most needs. One officer famously remarked, "If you don't control the dollars, you don't have a program." Many naval officers coming to Washington want to get close to the heartbeat of their warfare specialty. Fresh from the fleet, they want to work with such things as weapons requirements and programming. After all, they know something about what is needed and how it will be used. But there is another reason as well. Offices close to their warfare specialty are where the people are who will most help them before screening and promotion boards. So assignment to those offices tends to be personally satisfying and career-enhancing.

Nevertheless, do not overlook the shops that control the dollars for those systems you are most keen on getting into the fleet or for better maintaining those that are already there. Most crunches in Washington are dollar-related, just as most problems in your household are likely to be. Get close to the dollars, and you will get close to making things happen. I have in mind the comptroller and budget shops that are spread throughout the Washington headquarters scene. Detailers underline the point that the Navy does place great emphasis on money-related billets, and they cite telling evidence from their tours as recorders for command screening boards. You may not have an MBA, but learning and exercising the principles of fiduciary management are important in any line of work. Our Navy is not going anywhere without the dollars to pay the bills, including your paycheck.

The Importance of the Job Title

Some people argue that the title of the job makes the person, but this is not true. And some think too hard on the code and title before seeking the position, instead of carefully considering the position description. The code N1 is the deputy chief of naval operations, the chief of naval personnel—a three-star position.[2] An officer assigned to N130C might think of the extra numbers and letter C as too far removed from the position of influence. But N130C is the office that sets policy for Navy pay and allowances. Whatever the designation, we should all be interested in the Navy placing the right persons in the N130C office.

The lesson is: listen carefully when a detailer talks of a billet on the basis of a grand-sounding title or code, or on the basis that the job calls for an officer in the next senior grade. Likewise, be wary if told that you were handpicked for the job or faced tough competition to become the favored one. As oft stated, do your homework, call the incumbent, talk to your mentor, and give a Pentagon position careful consideration.

Family Life and Social Life

Officers coming to Washington for their first tour are surprised at the change in the social scene compared to their last command. Most offices have little social life except for an occasional "hail and farewell." Departing colleagues are usually honored at a lunch, if at all. Nevertheless, there are some social opportunities that are both fun and a help in getting known. These are the various festivities sponsored by the separate warfare communities, the annual Navy Relief Ball, class reunions for Naval Academy graduates at nearby Annapolis, and gatherings by graduates of civilian universities that have a Washington alumni chapter. Unfortunately, the Pentagon community resides in the District of Columbia and into the far reaches of Virginia and Maryland (some commute from as far away as West Virginia), so opportunities for a service-oriented social life are more limited than you enjoyed in the fleet. It is well worthwhile from both a personal enjoyment and a professional advancement standpoint to keep up your social connections and get a change of pace from the office atmosphere.

The advantages of Washington duty, and living in the commuting regions, include exceptional school districts, access to national historical and educational institutions, national-level celebrations, and local communities that are populated with like-minded military and government service employees. Most of your civilian neighbors will not know what you do, but they will appreciate your service and be understanding of the hardships associated with the Washington duty.

Reflections of Pentagon Service

In the book *Naval Officer's Guide to the Pentagon*, Vice Adm. Doug Crowder is introduced to share his insight on duty at the Pentagon. Retiring as a vice admiral, he completed ten Pentagon tours; his final position was deputy chief of naval operations for operations, plans, and strategy (N3/N5). These are items of advice for the more junior officer that can be applied to any command position but that may be more important in the Pentagon environment.

- **Hit the Deck Running:** Have your life and family settled before showing up for work, as you will immediately be considered the "expert" for the code that you are assigned.
- **Don't Join the "Bitching Class":** Work at the Pentagon will be a new challenge, and the incessant complaining about the desk duty versus sea duty can be disheartening and discouraging. Make the effort to be positive and reflective on how this duty is impacting your future sea duty.
- **Learn the Ropes:** The Pentagon duty and environment will require a steep learning curve. Sign up for the action officer

course, sit in on divisional meetings to observe the interaction of codes, and take the time to walk the halls to learn the codes and names of important players.
- **Personal Relationships:** Invest the time to do this early on.
- **When Briefing, Less Is More:** While PowerPoint is a normal way of business, learn to brief without PowerPoint or notes.
- **Civilians Serve, Too:** Respect them for their service and lean on their years of experience. They will be there long after you are gone.
- **What Language Are You Speaking?** Know your audience and use the appropriate vocabulary and tone.
- **Expand Your Horizons:** Attend various speaker sessions or discussion groups to look at broader defense issues that may impact your job or future commands.
- **If You Don't Understand Congress, You Really Don't Understand Washington:** The legislative affairs office will be your lifeline to providing the necessary response and support for congressional committees.
- **The Tank:** This is where key decisions are made for the Department of Defense. You won't be invited to attend, but you should have access to the schedule of discussion subjects, and they could be a touchpoint for you to request attendance.
- **The Power of Ideas:** "The Building really runs on the power of ideas. . . . Critical thinking and the ability to articulate your ideas both verbally and in writing are key skills that will make you a most valuable member of the team."[3]

Considering the detailer's triad, a tour in the Pentagon may lean more heavily toward your career needs than to the needs of the Navy or your personal preferences. Hopefully, this chapter gives you more to consider: is this the good hard job that you need to accept?

12

CAREER TRACKS FOR THE UNRESTRICTED LINE

> There is something conceptual, almost mathematically pure about life at sea—and at the same time hard and real which engages one more deeply and demands greater responsibility than is needed on land.
>
> —Goran Schildt, *In the Wake of the Witch*

A career in the Navy is built on the rotation between sea and shore duty stations that continues to give you the experience and ability to accept and perform in the next position of higher authority and responsibility. Governed by statutory limitations on length of service, the Navy is very much an "up or out" organization that must maintain the pipeline of officers promoting to fill all the fleet and shore positions of increased authority and responsibility. The importance for the individual officer is to realize you cannot stay for long in the position where you are now experienced and comfortable. To stay in the Navy, you will have to be available for additional duties that make you promotable and more valuable to the institution.

Naval officers, in their community legacy career path, follow four obligatory stops on the road to promotion in the unrestricted line: one or more sea tours as a junior officer, a sea tour as a department head (DH) of a ship or squadron, a command at sea, usually in the grade of commander preceded by an XO tour, and a major command at sea or ashore while serving in the grade of captain. The first sea tour may be split with two ship tours or consist of a single extended ship or squadron tour. During these early tours, officers learn the trade of going to sea, flying, or both. They typically serve as junior division officers and division officers. Surface warfare officers (SWOs), including nuclear-trained SWOs, earn basic warfare qualifications as an officer of the deck or other watch officer afloat. They then must earn the surface warfare pin in a timely manner and start the journey to qualification as a DH. Submarine officers have much the same path but must also qualify as a Navy nuclear engineer (a process that nuclear-trained SWOs also go through). Aviation junior officers qualify in all aspects of flying their aircraft, including various types of weapons delivery. Patrol plane aviators qualify for the coveted patrol plane commander designation.

Either toward the end of your junior officer tour or while you are on post-tour shore duty, your record will be reviewed by a community administrative board and you will be "screened" (meaning selected) for DH duty. The process may include a first and second look, but in general, the vast majority of warfare-qualified junior officers screen for DH. Failing to pass through this major wicket due to performance or disciplinary issues will certainly end your career aspirations.

The second major sea tour occurs in the grade of senior lieutenant or lieutenant commander. Surface warfare officers attend the DH course at the Surface Warfare Officers School in Newport, Rhode Island, and submarine officers attend the submarine officer advanced course at the Submarine School in Groton, Connecticut. The objective is to prepare for a meaningful sea tour serving as a department head afloat, leading larger groups of Sailors and honing a higher level of tactical skill. During this tour, DHs formally qualify for afloat command and also get a better idea of what command is like. Competition among officers serving in their DH tours is intense, as peer rankings and recommendations for promotion from your CO and your parent squadron are critical to screening for command just a few years down the road.

Aviators and surface warfare officers screen for command either during or soon after completing their DH tours. After serving on a shore duty, they will begin the command pipeline and prepare to take over an afloat command as XO first, then as CO. This is known as the XO-CO fleet-up model. Submarine officers must screen for XO separately and will serve as XO for a tour before being selected as CO.

Assignment to command in the grade of commander is critical to your future. In that command, you will compete against a peer group of your fellow COs, all of whom will have survived as tough a screening process as you. You will need a successful sea command tour in the grade of commander to be promoted to captain and will need to rank favorably against your peers in order to screen for major command.

The fourth or fifth sea tour is usually the major command tour, either at sea or ashore. Major sea commands include amphibious, destroyer, and submarine squadrons; aircraft carriers and air wings; cruisers; and major amphibious and service force ships or squadrons. For many captains, there is a bias toward afloat major command, but because there are important commands ashore that need quality skippers, some of the best officers qualifying for major command fill them instead. These commands include major naval stations (such as Norfolk, Pearl Harbor, Kings Bay, San Diego, etc.), naval air stations (such as Oceana, Pensacola, North Island, etc.), and some of the major schoolhouses. A major command is the capstone of a warfare officer's career. Only the best captains are selected to fill them, and they compose the pool from which flag officers are picked. At this point, other COs and flag officers can readily see the differences in performance of the commands and the commanders.

At each step of this progression of sea duty from junior officer afloat to major command afloat, a premium is placed on serving on an operational platform, especially conducting an overseas deployment. Better yet is a deployment that involves contingency or combat operations. You want to be tested and found able, and selection boards place great store on superior performance in tough circumstances. Not everyone is fortunate enough to get a deployment or a contingency operation or to see combat on their sea tours, and selection and screening boards recognize that service. Starting with the 1991 Gulf War and through the global war on terrorism, there was an increased and extended rotation of ships and squadrons to the U.S. Central Command area of responsibility. Additionally, during this extended period of conflict there were many individual augmentation (IA) assignments from all active and reserve communities, sending personnel to serve in combat roles in Iraq or Afghanistan or command staff billets in Djibouti or Bahrain. These IA positions were not part of any normal career path and yet in the end are considered highly at promotion boards. If you did not see active service during an overseas conflict, it was not a mark against you, but if you did so serve and do well, it was a plus on your record.

The entire subject of serving in overseas deployments, participating in contingencies, and seeing combat (and doing well) is one of the few aspects of a naval career that is heavily dependent on chance. To some degree, your future is decided by the conduct of the nation's adversaries. That said, you should actively seek assignment to a unit that is or will be deployed during your afloat tours.

While an operational deploying sea command might be preferable for most officers to better learn the tactical aspects of their community, the reality today is that many platforms will conduct shipyard periods for either minor or extensive repairs or upgrades. This time can be equally fruitful from a professional development standpoint, as there are many aspects to your platform's design or construction that are not accessible or apparent while waterborne or in a deployable condition, and becoming the expert on your platform is part of your job (and many old Sailors will tell you that you never know a ship as well as you know your first ship). If you are on a command that will spend an extended period of time in a shipyard or other availability, it is in your best interests to actively seek to supplement the crew of an operational command in order to conduct your qualifications and training. Typically, your command will support you in this, because it will ultimately benefit the command to have as much experience as possible when leaving the yards, but it still requires you to proactively seek those opportunities by communicating with your parent squadron and your waterfront shipmates.

The First Shore Tour

Between the obligatory sea tours described above, you will serve on a shore command in order to broaden your experience base and gain some much-needed normalcy, and there are a surprising number of possible shore duties, depending on your community. As discussed earlier, for most junior officers, a tour at the Naval Postgraduate School in Monterey, California, is likely an option. It is a great place to go to dig deeply into your favorite subjects while enjoying a great location, but many choose not to go there because it will not provide a "competitive" FITREP like you would get at an operational command. For aviators, the first shore tour might involve instructor duty in the training command, fleet replacement squadron, or another flying billet. A fortunate and able few may be assigned to test pilot school or the Blue Angels. Surface and submarine offices on their first shore tour might be instructors in a schoolhouse (e.g., SWO School, Sub School, Flight School, etc.), or as Reserve Officers Training Corps instructors at colleges and universities. Junior officers on their first tour ashore might find themselves in fleet staff positions, waterfront support positions, at overseas joint commands, or in Washington.

The Second Shore Tour

Your second shore tour is very important, as it will provide an opportunity to leverage your leadership and technical development over the course of your DH tour. There will be many possible shore duties within your technical area, such as inspection teams, squadron staffs, and larger operational staffs, but there will also be the higher likelihood and encouragement to serve in Washington. A tour as a relatively junior officer in Washington can be helpful in preparing you for later and critically important tours in your career. If you go to Washington, you should strive for assignment to an important shop with a history of being led by the Navy's brightest officers. One thing to consider is a joint tour. You must complete a qualifying joint tour and finish joint professional military education (JPME) phases I and II in order to be eligible for flag officer selection, so it is worth trying to get your joint tour complete on this tour (or, for submariners, after an XO tour) because getting a joint tour after command is harder to do (fewer billets are available to the different communities, and also a larger demand signal for "in-rate" expertise might keep you within your community). Your post-DH shore duty can be very important in helping to set you up for enhanced career potential, so take the right amount of time to review all options and talk with your mentors before finalizing your preferences.

A War College Tour

At some point just before or just after your third shore tour, you may consider attending one of the service war colleges. If it fits your career plan and if you aspire to flag rank, a professional military education tour at one of the war colleges is highly preferred. There are numerous online options for the defense colleges, but being there in person, rubbing elbows with the other service leaders, will build your résumé and your joint network. As important as the PME ticket is, keep your attention on your goal. You must screen for that commander command to progress, and your tour sequence to get there is your most important near-term objective. If you feel crowded at this point, with too much to do and not enough time to do it, you are in good company!

The Third Shore Tour

At this point you are serving as a senior commander or a newly selected captain and should be in one of the Washington-area system command (SYSCOM) headquarters or in a valued staff position. The warfare communities have a large number of post-command billets they have to fill at fleet concentration areas, at joint commands, and overseas. This tour is where you leverage your performance as CO to get you to one of the community-valued positions so you can continue to remain visible within and outside of your community. This will also quite possibly be the first shore duty where you are doing a job that is very different from your normal, operational job, but branching out will prepare you for the joint operational environment that you will be a part of as a senior officer.

Later Shore Tours

Later shore tours are clearly for the more seasoned officers, but junior officers might want to see what options and expectations do lie downstream. The senior readers may find yourselves in Washington after having successfully completed your major command tour. Many believe that, to really be in the flag race, you must—in addition to having excelled in a major command (typically meaning having been ranked as the number-one early promote in a competitive FITREP cycle)—have also served in a very demanding and visible shore or sea staff billet. These billets include (but are not limited to): key post–major command billets on the staffs of the CNO, the Navy Personnel Command, and the systems commands; key billets with the Joint Chiefs of Staff; commandant of midshipmen at the Naval Academy; chief of staff to the commanders of the numbered fleets; executive assistant to any four-star officer of any service; and any flag billet being filled with a captain for an extended period.

Billets that seem to not qualify under this criterion (but probably should) are chief of staff to type commanders and destroyer, submarine, carrier, and amphibious groups; most principle division head captain billets in the recruiting command; and some captain jobs overseas. Of course, as in any such listing, there are exceptions, but the odds of making flag get even longer when your comparative performance or assignment preferences place you in billets outside the mainstream. Those who make flag after an unconventional career are the subject of much attention within the service. Most officers admire the career stories of those who survived the rigors of paths less traveled and came out near the top of our profession.

Flag Shore Tours

If you are a newly selected flag officer, you probably were selected based on performance in your current shore tour or while serving in your major command. You are most likely in Washington or soon will be. Now you are benefiting from previous tours in or near the nation's capital or in outlying headquarters. This is an apprentice flag tour for you, and you may already be looking to return to sea for an all-too-brief stint as a group commander afloat with your own personal flag flying from the truck (top of the mast).

What is important for Navy admirals to understand is that from here on, your detailing and all flag matters are handled by an office in the Pentagon, with the director of flag management and detailing reporting to N1 (Navy Manpower and Personnel). Of importance to some and interest to many, the flag management and detailing office posts a monthly roster of Navy flag officers.[1] The recorded lineal number has importance in Navy honors, and the listed date of reporting gives some sights on potential rotation dates.

This chapter uses a very broad brush to paint a picture of what a career progression might entail and admittedly misses many of the details in waypoints and milestones expected in a successful career. A naval career is a long journey, and being successful requires stamina and a problem-solving mindset. Sailor or aviator skills are important in the earlier years of a career. As you get more senior, however, leading, managing, planning, motivating, innovating, and integrating become the most important talents. Savvy junior officers see life and their career as a continuum of change. There is life after a career of flying and ship driving is over. Enjoy it now, but recognize that eventually, the enterprise will require that you grow to lead it—not just fly it or sail it.

My closing instruction, especially for the junior officers, is that the detailers have refined their community briefs and made them readily available online for your study and consideration. Make their sites on MyNavy HR your first source of current helpful information, and then make the rounds and calls to get the best advice on what your career map should look like. One last personal observation: everyone does not fit the detailer's model. There can be many ways to the goals that you have set; there are alternative ways to the top; yet any primary or alternative route will require your sustained superior performance.

13

PROMOTION TO FLAG RANK

> From now on, you will always eat well and you will never hear the truth again.
>
> —Note in a congratulatory letter to a rear admiral (lower half) select

For junior officers who have traveled this far, any discussion of flag promotions must seem unreal. You just got here, and already I am talking about the end of a career! Moreover, most of you entered the Navy for reasons other than promotions. You are to be congratulated for your motivations, but now that you are here, you cannot help looking around you and saying, "Why not me?" Or perhaps you have been in long enough to say, "If I were the admiral (or the CNO), I would correct this or that." Again, congratulations! You see rank and promotions as a way to get good things done. The longer you stay in, the more the prospect of promotion will appeal you. You should pause occasionally and take the long view of your career—but as I said in the last chapter, do not overdo it.

In the Navy, the rank of admiral is certainly a rarified position. Admirals have distinction in their uniforms that include more "scrambled eggs" on their cover, gold on their shoulders, and stars on the collar, and whether they reach one-, two-, three-, or four-star rank, they will be (and will always be) addressed as "admiral." The promotion is life-changing. Others will address you and treat you differently. You may get the big corner office and may be accompanied by a supporting staff that manages your calls, calendar, and meetings. Or you may get the call to immediately move to (or back to) the Pentagon, where the A-ring office and hectic routine hardly seem appropriate for a newly promoted admiral. But everyone recognizes that there is something very special for reaching the rank of admiral in our Navy. Being in the right place at the right time, being fortunate for having the right experience or expertise, or just being lucky that there is a current gap that only you can fill gets you into the selection race, but it is the demonstrated superior performance in your captain role that tips the scales. And be ready to live in the "fishbowl," where your personal and professional behavior is carefully scrutinized and you will be expected to make the hard right answers. Be ready, for as Spider-Man says: "With great power (and authority) comes great responsibility."[1]

Many officers have little interest in promotion to flag even when they are well along in their naval careers. Others looking into their mirrors confess to themselves that they are not cut out for the job. Moreover, the sacrifices needed to stay in the race are not all that attractive to them. Others, and perhaps a majority, are so enamored of the mechanics and the here and now of the profession—shiphandling, flying, leading enlisted personnel, going to sea, visiting foreign ports, the adventure of change in duty station, and so on—that they have little time to consider promotion except when the lack thereof means shortening a personally rewarding career. For them, promotion to the rank of captain seems the pinnacle of their naval service. The simple arithmetic of the promotion pyramid means we need officers like those just described. They do the heavy lifting on the deck plates and in the hangars and the other day-to-day work of making the Navy function. There is nothing wrong with not aspiring to flag rank—or to captain, for that matter. In the last chapter of this book, we will examine the importance of knowing yourself and your capabilities, interests, and limitations. But here we look at how the Navy selects its top leadership.

Most of the captains I have encountered over a full career were fully qualified for flag rank. I consider these able captains, particularly those who had held a major command, to be the real backbone of the naval service. The fact that they did not make flag rank was a matter of numbers, not qualifications. As a captain about to retire, you may look back on a productive, honorable, and even glorious career. When you return to civilian life, it is enough that you served honorably as a captain in the Navy to warrant the respect and admiration of your new neighbors, old friends, and former shipmates.

For those still left in the race for flag, the hard work and dedicated service continue. The competition is very keen; roughly only one in one hundred captains will be selected for flag rank. Other than the competition and the odds, what makes promotion to flag rank different? What is the flag board looking for that is so different from consideration for promotion to the more junior ranks? And are you ready to move and fill the gap for the needs of the Navy?

Perhaps the biggest difference is that there are relatively few flag billets—measured in the several hundreds rather than thousands of captain's billets.[2] Thus, the flag board in selecting has a very precise idea of the needs of the service. If there is any doubt on that score, the flag board receives specific guidance from the convening authority, the Secretary of the Navy, and information from the chief of naval personnel on the billets to be filled.[3] Although all selection boards attempt to gauge the probable future performance of the officers being considered, the flag board takes this task even more seriously than the others. They are selecting the members of the board of directors of the Navy—officers who will lead the Navy at sea and ashore, officers who will put in place the systems and personnel with which the Navy will fight over several future decades, perhaps as long as half a century.

Another difference in the selection of flag officers is that the officers selected must demonstrate a different type of leadership. To this point officers under consideration have commanded individual ships, squadrons, and relatively small tactical formations below strike groups in size. But those selected for flag will command battle groups, battle forces, and eventually battle fleets. Some of them will have major responsibilities in the shore establishment and control billions of dollars and thousands of personnel. They must command or manage through multiple echelons, not a few departments and a somewhat larger number of divisions. They must show promise in being able to develop policies and manage operations that flow through many others while setting the tone for the whole. In addition, they must be able to work effectively with other offices in and outside the Department of Defense. As flag officers, the scope of their duties will expand both horizontally and vertically.

Most of the time, the board picks good operators. The officers are good shiphandlers, "good sticks" (the aviation expression), good with Sailors, and good at keeping their bosses happy. Even with these qualifications, though, some will not measure up to the level of skill needed to manage and lead truly large enterprises. Their valuable expertise is largely limited to the unit level. With this danger in mind, the flag selection board must extrapolate from the records before them to pick those who will best handle these expanded responsibilities. There is an important point to be reiterated here. A fitness report jacket is a log of past accomplishments and shortcomings and is not by itself a predictor of the future. Thus, the flag board is less interested in how good a shiphandler you were (they expect you to have that skill) than in the even better decision-maker you may become. They are looking for clues in your jacket as to your potential to grow into very demanding duties and responsibilities.

You might respond, "Is that not what all promotion boards are looking for?" The answer is yes. But flag boards are different because they are picking the people who will lead and command the whole enterprise called the U.S. Navy. Mistakes made by lesser boards can inflict damage on the institution, but bad flag picks strike the institution at its foundations. So, this is serious business.

Specific Characteristics Required

What specifically is the flag board looking for? The short answer is: a group of relatively young leaders who will help the current flag community pull the Navy's wagon. They are looking not for show horses, but for workhorses. They want people who got things done wherever they served. They want people with supple minds, who can represent the Navy within the Department of Defense, before Congress, and to the American people, and who can confound our enemies. Good operational skills are a given, though occasionally the board will select a few officers with very specialized skills that outweigh any lack of sparkle in their operational résumé.

Other skills are also sought. The board is looking for people who know the system and the book but also know that flag officers occasionally need to go outside the system or the book to get things done. The trick is to know when such initiatives are needed. Rockers, shakers, and movers are in. Personal empire builders and political officers are out, and smart, aggressive problem solvers are in.

Now the question to ask yourself is: what are the specifics they will be looking for in my jacket or in what others say about me? I suggest the following:

1. A good, solid grounding in the basics of the naval profession (professional competence). The board wants to see strong performance in command, particularly a major command afloat or ashore. They will cut through the nice words (a lot have them) in the jacket and look for solid facts and data to back up your accomplishments. Good combat performance will catch their eye, but their major concern will be to see that you perform well under the pressure of events. Do you know your stuff? Should you be trusted with a group command afloat?
2. The intangibles of character—honor, courage, and commitment, to use the popular phrase. Can you be trusted to do the right thing? Have you been tested? Are you stable, persistent, and gutsy?
3. A demonstrated potential for professional growth to fill positions of greatly increased responsibility. Could you lead other potential selectees? Would you be comfortable and effective in a realm of greatly expanded span and depth of control?
4. A team player. Are you a loose cannon or one who works well with a variety of constituencies? The board is not looking for Mr. or Ms. Personality, but loners and self-serving types need not apply.
5. A suppleness of mind. Although smarts are prized, mental agility and constructive imagination anchored in reality are even more valuable. A variant of this trait is situational awareness—an ability to see the forest and the trees at the same time and devise a path through them that confronts or circumvents obstacles, each at the appropriate time.
6. Needs of the service. Is it likely that you would become a detailing problem? Where would you best serve in our Navy? Have you had your joint tour yet, or will we have to send you to a joint billet first? Have you been in Washington recently? Was the job a key one?
7. Service reputation. The board cannot read everything about the prospective selectee, no matter how complete or well written the

jacket is. How well known by reputation are you to the board? What do people outside your warfare community say about you? Have you "stovepiped" your career (that is, stayed mostly in your warfare community, passing through a succession of billets in that specialty, to grease the skids before screening and promotion boards), or are you a broad-gauge officer who is well known in the service and not dependent on your warfare community connections?

These seven tests are not written down in a checklist and put before the board, but you can be sure that each board member goes through a calculus that involves all or most of these factors.

The Perspective of the President of the Board

The president of the promotion selection board, as well as individual members, wants to pick the best applicant to meet the needs of the service. But the president has some additional concerns. That individual must see that the board's selectees as a group satisfy the guidance of the convening authority. The president is, of course, limited at the outset by the number of officers who can be selected. Still, if the convening authority suggests the need for some specific specialties or emphasizes certain types of experience, the president must make an effort to see that the board's results reflect that guidance. The last thing the president wants is for the Secretary of the Navy to reject the board's list of selectees or remove a selectee from it (for cause).

In addition to following the guidance, the president of the board wants to ensure that specific warfare communities are fairly treated and represented in the final list. The president is constantly aware that only the best must be selected but knows fairness is an important factor if the Navy is to retain top-flight officers in all communities. The results of the board will be scrutinized closely by every captain and by most others in the service. Did the selectees have a successful major command, a demanding Washington job? Which subcategories in the warfare communities fared best (e.g., air wing commanders versus carrier skippers, cruiser skippers versus destroyer squadron commodores, and amphibs versus cruiser/destroyer types)? How many selectees had advanced degrees? How many were graduates of service colleges? The questions, though they move into the realm of seemingly trivial distinctions, are ones of keen interest to one or more professional communities.

In a sense, the flag board results indicate the seriousness of the Navy's leadership by its fairness in considering for promotion officers with differing professional backgrounds, their image of the future Navy, and their sense of the needs of the service. This message reverberates through the service. It exposes potential embarrassments when we do not follow our own exhortations to the service (for example, we say the contributions of a specific community are important but then deny them proportionate representation on the promotion lists).

Now for a few words about perceptions versus facts. When they are selected for flag rank, many officers are serving in executive assistant (to very senior flag officer or departmental officials) billets when the list is released. In almost all cases, they have already had a successful major command tour. But often that fact is obscured by the focus on the selectee's current assignment. The impression is given that, to make flag, serving in an executive assistant billet is the key to preference. In almost all cases, it is the other way around: the officer is in an executive assistant billet because of past superior performance, including in a major command billet.

Youth versus Age

The Navy as an institution would dearly like to have the issue of youth versus age both ways. They would like the person to have the time in a career to fill all the boxes—get a postgraduate education, go to the war colleges, and get plenty of sea time and demanding Washington duty. They would like the officer to fit in a joint tour, have longer command tours, have more homesteading opportunities, and so on. At the same time, there is pressure to promote the best earlier and hurry them to flag rank by a rapid passage through numerous qualifying billets. This pressure has been accelerated under the Defense Officer Personnel Management Act and subsequent officer personnel legislation. Under current rules, the vast majority of officers retire at the thirty-year point (or earlier), and only a few flag officers go on to the thirty-five-year point and beyond. Rapid promotion is a key factor in the retention of the best and brightest. Therefore, it should not surprise us that some flag officers today have what in an earlier age would have been called incomplete résumés. On the plus side, they are much younger and can spend more time in the flag ranks.

Occasionally, a Secretary of the Navy will become involved in this issue and caution selection boards that maturity and experience also have some value in the drive for youth and vigor. You should be aware of these crosscurrents and the trade-offs. Many believe the current balance is about right. There is room for older— and younger—flag officers, and a wise flag board is not bound by stereotypes.

In spite of the imperfections that persist in the flag selection system, it is fair by almost any standard. More work still needs to be done in seeing that smaller or less influential warfare communities receive an appropriate number of flag selections, but progress is being made. In industry, the top jobs frequently go to protégés (or relatives) of the powerful, to lateral entries as opposed to bottom-up candidates, and to those who have done very well in their most immediate past position. The naval service has few peacetime indices as concrete as the financial bottom line that characterizes the business world. The Navy's bottom line is to win. Moreover, the service demands attention to the intangibles that in business are often put aside as secondary factors (such as staff turnover, morale, grooming qualified successors in management, and quality of product at the margin).

What are the lessons for junior officers just starting their career? The organization is basically fair, but the training and assignment pipeline (designator and warfare platform) you enter can have a major impact on your promotion to the senior grades. The common elements on each step of the path upward are top performance in your current job, preparing to take over your boss's job in good time, and staying as close as you can to the mainstream of the naval profession—going to sea with the combat forces.

14

AWARDS AND DECORATIONS

A soldier will fight long and hard for a bit of colored ribbon.

—Napoleon

You may find that the above quote does not line up well with much of what is to be considered in the following text. Napoleon was generously using awards as a motivation for his troops and even declared, "Give me enough medals and I'll win you any war!" In contrast, today the purpose of Department of the Navy (DON) military awards is to recognize limited but deserving service members for acts of heroism, exceptionally meritorious achievement or service, and arduous or otherwise special service.[1] The awards are not promised or guaranteed, and while presentation of the awards brings special attention to the awardee, the overall impact of wearing ribbons remains most important to the individual and their community group.

There was an era when the Navy issued few decorations. The Navy as an institution was very proud that its dress tunics had no adornment except the stripes of rank: few medals, no warfare or professional badges, and few service ribbons. That custom started to change during World War I, when campaign ribbons emerged and the first warfare badges were instituted, beginning with the Submarine Warfare pin in 1923. It was not uncommon to see a senior officer with just two or three service ribbons. Few medals were awarded in that period between the world wars, and most senior officers wore no more than their stripes of rank and the Great War (World War I) victory ribbon.

After World War II and its perceived "medal mania," there was a push within the Navy's leadership to return to the more restrained practices of the 1920s and 1930s. Award recommendations were often downgraded or returned to the sponsoring command with a terse comment to include the citation in the officer's next fitness report. In the post-Vietnam era, medals became even scarcer as the overarching theme was: if you haven't been in the combat theater, you could not have had the experience of arduous or otherwise meritorious service. But this draconian policy did not survive long, particularly when it collided with the much more liberal policies of the other services. The Navy found that it could not turn the clock back alone.

As the Cold War wore on, there was a new profusion of service ribbons and even more classes of medals. Additionally, joint service medals were added to parallel the services' own awards structures. Then, in the past twenty years of conflict in Iraq and Afghanistan, the Navy continued to readily recognize the individual's participation in the theater of conflict. In a single operation, a service member could receive a personal military decoration, a unit decoration, and a campaign, expeditionary, and service medal, all to recognize the individual and unit participation in a significant military operation.[2] Before 2001 most of the new Navy awards were given more for meritorious service in normal operations, either in port or at sea, than for action in combat. The combat "V" is included with some Navy medals (for example, the Navy Commendation Medal, the Bronze Star, and the Legion of Merit) to make it clear that the award (often awarded for noncombat performance) was for actions against the enemy.[3]

The *Navy and Marine Corps Awards Manual* lays out the criteria and eligibility for all the awards, and the expectation is that the citations and supporting documentation clearly meet the criteria for the awards. The manual highlights the way awards were normally or historically calibrated to every level of performance and even rank. For example, the Navy Achievement Medal (NAM) is often awarded for performance by a junior officer or enlisted Sailor. Navy Commendation Medals (COMs) are often awarded to O-4s for performance in their middle-level management positions, and Meritorious Service Medals (MSMs) are often awarded for performance in O-5 billets. Distinguished Service Medals (DSMs) are limited by common usage to senior flag officers—usually at the end of tour or on retirement. Today, a Legion of Merit (LOM) is normally awarded to officers, typically O-6s, in principal commands ashore or lesser commands at sea, whereas in the past, usually just flag officers were given that award.

At one time, awards and decorations were a factor in promotion because they were rare. Today, the number and sheer quantity of awards have resulted in officer screening and promotion boards not paying much attention to them (unless they are of exceptionally high level, like an O-4 or O-5 receiving a Bronze Star).[4] Today, end-of-tour awards for department heads and more senior superior performing officers are the norm. The awards are nice to have, but they are worth less than good fitness reports, though they often parallel them.

This award inflation has resulted in relatively junior officers and petty officers wearing two, three, or even four rows of ribbons. The perceived morale payoff for this proliferation works toward making this dilution worth the price (and Napoleon would agree!). Award ceremonies provide an excellent opportunity to recognize publicly an officer's or Sailor's contribution to the command—something that is impossible with the confidential fitness report. Even more importantly, it can provide an opportunity for family members to observe and participate in this recognition, which can be a very powerful motivational tool.

It is worth noting that, while officers do not necessarily get a promotion benefit for normal awards, your enlisted Sailors do receive promotion points for awards above a certain level (e.g., no points for a commanding officer's letter of commendation, but one point for a flag-level or senior executive service letter of commendation, and two points for a Navy Achievement Medal). Recognizing your Sailors' performance by recommending them for awards has a very concrete result—they could promote faster and make more money, which they will certainly appreciate.

Recent discussions with senior active duty officers reflect that selection and screening boards do not pay much attention to awards and decorations unless extraordinary circumstances (usually bravery in action) are involved. A Silver Star, a Navy Cross, and, of course, the Medal of Honor are noted positively. Indeed, Navy Cross and Medal of Honor winners are notable for the rest of their career and admired by their comrades in arms, and sometimes this halo effect carries over to promotion boards. Nonetheless, most senior and retired officers know that many highly decorated naval heroes have not always fared well before such boards. This is not because they did not deserve their decorations but because there is much more to a successful career than serving bravely and well in combat. Some purists may bemoan this fact, arguing that the services are organized and trained for combat and that it is silly not to reward (and promote) those who have been tested in combat and performed well. But they confuse promotions predicated on future service leadership requirements with rewards and awards presented in recognition for past service.

The most important part of wearing medals and campaign ribbons has nothing to do with performance and promotion. Rather, such awards are a tangible demonstration of the wearer's sea and air service in the conflicts, campaigns, special missions, and so forth. The campaign and battle stars and combat "Vs" tell the story of active service and identify a band of brothers and sisters with solid bonds to each other, their service, and their country. You should not take your awards too seriously. If they come your way, accept them graciously and wear them proudly, but understand that it is more important for you to receive an outstanding (for example, "early promote") competitive fitness report (meaning a FITREP that ranks you against your peers). Awards are the Navy's way of providing visible recognition of superior performance. Your lack of decorations will not be a strike against you because those officers sitting on boards generally recognize that the awards system has had capricious periods, that you don't control the situations in which you serve, and that the awarding authorities vary widely in how readily they distribute awards. If you are worried that a peer of yours has more awards than you do, you are focusing on the wrong thing. Better to focus on ensuring your Sailors get the recognition they deserve, since it can actually make a difference in their lives.

An important reminder is that the misuse or misrepresentation of awards leads to trouble. In the past, some senior officers have been challenged and found at fault for wearing medals they had not received. Even worse are those who violate the Stolen Valor Act of 2013, which specifically makes it a crime to falsely claim military service, embellished rank, or earned awards with the intent to obtain money, property, or other tangible benefits. The bottom line is that you should wear your awards properly and proudly. They do reflect your important service to our Navy and nation. Just be sure that your chest of ribbons properly reflects the records in your service jacket.

A final consideration is that military awards and medals do carry significant emotional and motivational weight. The best is when everyone in the command acknowledges that the recognition and award are deserved for actions performed, and the commander makes an extended effort to publicly recognize the awardee. The worst is when awards are late, overinflated, or, conversely, lacking the appropriate level of recognition for heroism, achievement, service, and sacrifice.

15

PASS THE (SOCIAL) POLISH, PLEASE

> Good manners reflect something from inside—an innate sense of consideration for others and respect for self.
>
> —Emily Post

Of all the chapters in *Career Compass*, this one might reflect the greatest changes (and challenges) since the original printing almost twenty years ago. While it seems to me that the Navy, and the U.S. military in general, sets high standards for conduct and dress, the rules and regulations for uniform and protocol are regularly changing to accommodate the norms in our local societies. The Navy is a very structured organization, but it cannot be seen as a bastion that is ignorant of or impervious to the current social trends. So, you will see changes in the uniform regulations, grooming standards, correspondence formatting, rules for phone etiquette, agendas for "command" functions—up to the point that the changes negatively impact good order and discipline, or if they violate rule one from George Washington's *Rules of Civility and Decent Behavior in Company and Conversation*: "Every Action done in Company, ought to be with Some Sign of Respect, to those that are Present."[1]

This chapter is about something called social polish—a soft subject to those who might believe the fraternity antics of the film *Animal House* are the standard to be met in public and personal

Pass the (Social) Polish, Please

conduct. The topic includes more than "knife-and-fork" etiquette, a term that was associated with the old-school adage that knowing which fork to use first at a formal dinner was the first step in social graces. Social polish includes basic courtesy and consideration for others. You cannot be a gentleman or lady without it. You cannot be an effective military leader without it!

This book is not a volume on etiquette. Many such books exist, and most are good. The point here is that exercising social graces is a most valuable skill that facilitates and accentuates the previously mentioned attributes, which makes you a welcomed, valued member of any command organization. The best news is that the social graces comprise an art that can be learned if you were not fortunate enough to get that indoctrination early in your life. Hopefully, the high expectations set at your commissioning command have not been lost in your advancement through the fleet commands.

My observation, however, is that we, as a service, have not maintained the high expectations that are outlined in thoughtfully written books like *Service Etiquette*.[2] Bad manners are all around us. Simple good table manners seem to be a lost art in some wardrooms and in many restaurants. Although we mostly give our seniors the respect that is their due, our courtesy to other shipmates regardless of seniority borders on disrespectful. Today, our Navy faces the same challenges in this regard that the Royal Navy faced in the seventeenth century when it was alleged that its officers were not gentlemen and that its gentlemen were not sailors. We run the risk of a descent in our manners to the level of the popular cultural scene. The fact that the Navy is a service of young people, where peer pressure is a critical factor, makes our job to stop the ebb even harder.

Having social graces starts with knowing what the rules and expectations are and not ridiculing them as being only for the old and out of touch. It means you should not only have an etiquette book in your library but should also update yourself occasionally on its contents. The etiquette books from the Naval Institute Press and the Naval History and Heritage Command provide guidelines and the historical and practical perspective on why this is important to good order and discipline and, ultimately, the effective combat readiness of a command. These are more than reference books; they are a guide to daily conduct.

I can reflect on personal observations that made me very aware of, and the need to understand, the differences in acceptable and normal etiquette standards from one command to another. Stationed on a Navy cruiser in San Diego, our captain had his cabin, office, and mess distant from the officer's wardroom. The captain was very much "old school" and designated the dress code for command functions as "California casual," which he defined as coat and tie for men and dresses for women. Toward the end of my tour on the cruiser, we had a change of command, and the new CO was hosting a wardroom reception at his home. When questioned by the XO, the new CO encouraged everyone to come in "California casual." In a timely manner we were queued up at the front door, in jackets and ties, when the CO opened the door to welcome us in his version of "California casual"—cutoff jeans and flip-flops. So, know what the command expectations are. Additionally, for my follow-on tours stationed in Hawai'i, "local casual" was board shorts and flip-flops. And you learn that everyone hugs—more than shaking hands. Uniform regulations were regularly ignored to accommodate the heavy draping of lei and other flower adornments. Local Hawaiian etiquette was different, and a *haole* (non-native) had to learn to accept and practice the *kama'āina* (Hawaiian) norms.

Having social graces does mean more than dressing in the acceptable local garb; it is to demonstrate by your conduct that you respect others (Washington's rule one), avoid needless embarrassment, put people at ease, and present an appearance and demeanor that are respectful and attentive to what is going on about you. It means you should avoid the in-your-face confrontations and shouting matches, the put-down styles, and the me-first demeanor so often seen on television shows and in the movies. It does mean that you should be aware of your words and tone in company and conversation. Most modern situation comedies present good examples of how *not* to conduct yourself.

Why are these graces important components of a naval officer's seabag? The simple answer is that the more successful you are in your career, the more likely you will be in the public spotlight, and the more likely you will represent the U.S. Navy overseas and before the American public and its representatives. If your behavior is rough, uncouth, and grating and if your manners are uncivil, they will reflect adversely on you and the Navy. Consequently, when the Navy picks its future leaders, it pays some attention to the social polish of its candidates. It is not to your advantage to be described as "a bit rough around the edges," "a diamond in the rough," or "not suitable for polite company." Alas, this is not to say that everyone in the Navy's leadership has polished manners. Some manage to climb to the top without them, but their climb was made more difficult for their rough edges. And when those few get to the top, their lack of polish is a major disadvantage in gaining the respect of others for their office and their service.

How We Arrived Where We Are Today

The Navy of the nineteenth and first half of the twentieth century was an aristocratic service whose officers with few exceptions were schooled to have meticulous manners. Back then, almost all regular officers graduated from the Naval Academy, and that institution placed great emphasis on social polish. Conforming at the academy was the rule then as it is now, but the standard of social conduct was much higher than it has become at the academy, in the naval service, and in society as a whole. In those earlier days, you measured up—or else. With the great expansion of the Navy just before and during World War II, the service went through a major transformation, and most peacetime niceties and civilities went by the wayside. A war was on, and some of its first casualties were the social graces among the officer corps. Not only was the Naval Academy no longer the standard setter in such matters, but many if not most of the new officers brought on for the duration of the war had not finished their college education. Although a college education is not a guarantee of good manners, the experience exposes one to their practice. The wartime officers turned out to be good fighters, and much was forgiven for lapses in the social graces.

Post–World War II, the Navy was still very large, and the push was on to get all officers a college degree. An attempt was also made to resurrect the prewar system of instilling social graces among midshipmen at the Naval Academy. Table manners were emphasized, calls were made and returned, officers were not to be seen pushing baby strollers and using umbrellas, polite social conversation was nurtured, boisterous conduct was frowned upon, and junior officers were expected to be attentive to their seniors and not speak unless called on. But in civil society, the postwar assault on good manners overwhelmed even the Naval Academy. The 1960s created a bigger upheaval impacting the Navy standards. Being a "hippie" was very much the rage, and rioting against the military and rejecting established institutions and middle-class values were the norm. Today, with the proliferation and ubiquity of social media, influencers on the media platforms of YouTube and TikTok are having a significant impact on what is and (maybe) is not acceptable behavior and language in the public forum. As outlined in the Navy's Social Media Handbook: "As a Navy leader, you must lead by example. You must show your Sailors and Navy civilians that improper or inappropriate online behavior is not tolerated and must be reported if experienced or witnessed. When it comes to your position as command leadership, your conduct online should be no different from your conduct offline, and you should hold your Sailors and civilians to that same standard."[3]

We need to focus on the health of good manners at the entry points for the Navy, because if the academy, OCS, and NROTC units do not get it right, the chances are that the naval service will not do so either. Setting the tone for etiquette and courtesies at the service's officer accession programs is still one of their de facto missions. Be attentive in your first duty rotations to the habits you create and the behaviors you accept. Once you have set the bar too low in appearance and behavior, it will be much harder to raise it back up.

This brief look at the historical background is intended to make you more sensitive to where we were and where we are and to provide a personal and institutional incentive to hold the standards and push against any negative popular behavior. Social graces are one of the keys to your success in life—in service or in civilian life. You may still engage in the rough-and-tumble and give-and-take of the wardroom, the ready room, the athletic field, and the locker room while paying attention to how ladies and gentlemen behave. We kid a great deal about the point that we are officers and gentlemen or ladies by act of Congress. But if you overlook how we conduct ourselves, you will operate your entire career without an important skill.

By the time there is a need for a third edition of *Career Compass*, there will be the social pull to change (or relax) the current rules, regulations, and expectations for our naval personnel. Be critical only of rule changes that impact the good order and discipline or minimize the necessity to treat everyone with dignity and respect.

In the original edition of this book, Rear Admiral Winnefeld presented Ten Simple Rules for Social Acceptability (all were highlighted by George Washington and are still appropriate today):

1. Get an etiquette book and read it. Do it now. (Start with *Washington's Rules*.)
2. Be quiet and listen. Not everyone wants to hear what you have to say. Conversation among ladies and gentlemen is a multisided affair. Listening well is not only an official but also a social necessity (rule seventy-four).
3. Stand up. This elementary courtesy is the hallmark of a gentleman or lady when addressed by a senior in rank or age (rule twenty-eight).
4. Defer to others in social matters—in conversation, dining, and precedence. Make the effort to see that others are seated or served first, given the right-of-way, and so on (rule thirty-four).
5. Pay attention to what is going on around you. You might learn how to conduct yourself and learn what is required. Officers who are unaware are of no use to anyone and are a source of embarrassment to their shipmates (rule eighty-seven).
6. Pay attention to your grooming. You should wear a well-turned-out uniform and civilian clothing and maintain hair, nails, and basic body cleanliness (rule fifty-one).
7. Treat your associates as ladies and gentlemen (always—and even if they are not). Even one or two ladies or gentlemen in a group raise the tone of the gathering (rule one).
8. Do not draw attention to yourself—in dress, voice, or actions. Boisterous and exhibitionist behavior does not define the lady or gentleman (rule fifty-four).

9. Pay attention to your language. You should eliminate not only cursing and profanity but also the crudities in common usage: rough, trendy slang. Listen to what you are saying. If you use two to three "you know" expressions a minute in your speech, you have said too much (rule seventy-eight).
10. Do not complain or whine. If you cannot or will not change matters, do not comment on what is wrong with you or the world (rule 105).

These ten rules (plus the one hundred more in Washington's list), if scrupulously observed, would go a long way to make you a lady or gentleman—whatever the gaps in your upbringing or education or lapses caused by keeping rough company. You will quickly notice that these rules do not apply just to naval officers and might wonder what the connection is to your profession. Part of the answer was provided earlier: you will be a more respected representative of the Navy at home, abroad, and aboard ship if you are a lady or gentleman and are seen as such by your skippers. The rest of the answer lies in the effect that courteous behavior has on your relationships with your shipmates. You will find that friendship and comradeship come more easily, even with your enlisted men and women. Some of these individuals may be very crude in manner, but they know a gentleman or lady when they see one, and most instinctively react positively. They quickly perceive that you see beyond yourself and respect them as well. The best of them will want to emulate your behavior, and so an upward spiral in civility, mutual respect, and unit effectiveness occurs.

In a recent forum at the Naval Academy, a flag officer was asked, "How did you rise to the rank of admiral?" While the content of this book highlights many of the critical professional abilities and expectations for superior performance, the response was very much aligned with Washington's rule nineteen: "Let your Countenance be pleasant but in Serious Matters Somewhat grave."

16

THE NAVY SPOUSE AND FAMILY

> Navy Spouse—The Toughest Job in the Navy!
> —Popular T-shirt, challenge coin, and bumper sticker quote

On military spouse appreciation day in 2022, CNO Adm. Michael Gilday and his wife, Linda, sent this message to our Navy family: "Together, we applaud everything you do for your Sailor and the entire Navy family. We appreciate your service and do not take your sacrifice nor the challenges you face for granted. To my wife Linda—and to all of the incredible spouses around the world—Thank you."

Having addressed the impact of changing social norms previously, one of the more important considerations for our current and future Navy is the role of, and respect and accommodation for, a Navy spouse.[1] An officer's (or Sailor's) spouse might now be addressed as a partner and a marriage considered cohabitation. Removal of the Don't Ask, Don't Tell policy has opened the access to same-sex marriages; paternity and maternity leave policies give long-overdue support for new parents; and special programs are in place for adoptions, single parents, and special-needs dependents. Yet, it is important to understand that most of the rules in place to support the service member and their dependents have not changed. To have access to the privileges that come with military service, the spouse and dependents must be accounted for in the

The Navy Spouse and Family

Defense Enrollment Eligibility Reporting System (DEERS). A marriage or dependent status must be registered on the second page of the service jacket before the individual can be included in the register for a common access card (CAC), base privileges, and medical coverage, and to be included in PCS orders. While each officer should be attentive to their own official status (and updates for any changes along the way), this is a very important concern that needs to be regularly addressed for those subordinates in your chain of command.

Junior officer readers may be wondering why this subject is coming up at all. After all, they will note that so far, emphasis has been placed on professional performance. What does a spouse have to do with such performance? The answer to that question might be regularly answered in the text of almost every change of command or retirement ceremony, when the officer passionately (and often tearfully) thanks their spouse (and close family) for the continued support necessary to make the career a success. What does such support have to do with conning a ship, leading a division of enlisted personnel, or flying military aircraft? The answer to that and other such questions requires stepping back from the specific skills needed in the naval profession and looking at the people serving in submarines, in squadrons, and in the offices of the shore establishment both as human beings and as critical parts of what makes the Navy work.

Coaches have long known that top performance on the athletic field is keyed to eliminating distractions and fostering a supportive atmosphere in the athlete's family. Whereas there is game day for athletes, there are lengthy, dangerous training requirements and overseas deployments for naval officers who leave their families behind. An important part of the readiness equation is to have your spouses and your family adequately informed and supported—and supportive. Navy spouses themselves play an important role in meeting these requirements. If the family grows to include children, the Navy spouse will take on a primary care role, particularly when the service member spouse is deployed.

Every married Navy family can add value to this chapter as the career and family experiences vary so widely. Books like the *Navy Spouse's Guide* and the text and continuing blog of *Modern Military Spouses* chronicle the ups, downs, highlights, challenges, and advice for a successful family life, while transiting a successful Navy career.[2] For the best example of a Navy couple's devotion and persistence in the face of extreme trials, the story of Vice Adm. Jim Stockdale and Sybil Stockdale, *In Love and War*, is at the top of the reading list.[3]

Couples marry for various reasons, having various backgrounds and expectations. Yet, there are some common characteristics of Navy spouses that are helpful in achieving a positive balance between the professional career and a healthy, happy family. In the first edition of this book, Admiral Winnefeld presented this list of helpful characteristics—which my wife still considers appropriate and helpful.

1. Navy spouses should be blessed with a generally positive outlook and a friendly disposition. They need not be unconditionally optimistic, but they should be willing to give others and circumstances the benefit of the doubt.
2. Navy spouses should be flexible. They will encounter many changes in location and circumstances in their spouse's career. They should take pride in their ability to adapt and should also firmly advocate for their family when necessary.
3. Navy spouses should be problem solvers. Unexpected challenges are a fact of life in any family. But married life in the Navy involves

dealing with surprises (some unpleasant), occasionally with the spouse deployed and not available.
4. Navy spouses should be sociable and not isolate themselves from others. The wardroom and ready room comradery is often bolstered in social engagements, and with seniority comes the expectation of hosting such events.
5. Navy spouses should be caring and empathetic. Understanding and tending to the needs of their spouse is vital, and spouses will often be in a position of providing assistance to or receiving assistance from the families of the command while their spouses are deployed.
6. Navy spouses should respect their spouse's career and shipmates. Hopefully, they are not rebels or antiestablishment, but they need not be conformists either. They must be willing to subordinate their views and personal conduct in those areas where they interface with their spouse's naval duties and commitments.
7. Navy spouses should be prepared to make personal sacrifices to advance their spouse in the profession. As an example, spouses may have to uproot from their own personal career aspirations, school systems, and cherished neighborhoods to move when their spouse transfers to a new command.
8. Navy spouses should not wear their spouse's rank. Although they will enjoy a certain amount of deference and will routinely be treated with great courtesy, they should neither demand nor expect special consideration.
9. The Navy spouse should be your greatest champion, cheerleader, and teammate. As is regularly highlighted in farewell speeches, successful officers recognize the importance of positive support from the home front!

Sadly, the U.S. Census Bureau reports that military couples have the highest divorce rates of any career field and that the impact of the divorce can be especially hard on military families.[4] Do some service members fail to uphold their side of the relationship? Perhaps. Do some Navy spouses fail to meet these standards? Perhaps. It is better to look at it in terms of "fit." Spouses do not join the Navy, but they have the realities of service thrust upon them through their service member spouse. Some have a great deal of difficulty adjusting to family separations during overseas deployments, to what they see as a stifling hierarchy, to a certain loss of privacy and their own career pursuits, or to the need to move frequently. Others believe the potential financial advantages of civilian life and the business world outweigh the security that the service provides. Most are decent people whose spouse is in the wrong profession as far as they are concerned. In the end, the service member and their spouse are the final arbiters of whether a continued career in the Navy is a good fit for them as a couple and as a family. The best advice is to seek mentorship from other couples and families who seem to demonstrate the achievement of balance and satisfaction with the Navy way of life and its effect on the family. Considering this conversation during the dating phase is heartily advised!

Could an officer be promoted or fail of selection because of their spouse? Not directly. Fitness reports and selection boards do not allow mention of spouses whatsoever. In fact, a commanding officer or board member doing so would be swiftly corrected for such an action. Indirectly, any officer who is not able to achieve some kind of harmony between home and work will be likely to exhibit a decrease in the quality of their performance or have constraints on their assignments or deployability that could make them less competitive with their peers. Spouses have reputations just as their serving partners do. That is, spouses who are involved positively, have been a booster and a morale builder in the unit, and have a wide circle of Navy friends are real pluses, and their virtues

The Navy Spouse and Family

are known very widely throughout the service. When detailing an officer to an overseas or aide job, assignment officers may in some cases shade their recommendations for or against the candidate based on their knowledge of the family's dynamic reputation.

The principal impact of a spouse's suitability, however, is on the serving officers themselves. A supportive spouse is a priceless advantage in boosting an officer's self-confidence, ability to bring focus to the job and the command, and willingness to sign up for the sacrifices that are the hallmark of a successful career. It comes down to the commitment of the spouse to the serving officer and that officer's commitment to a lifetime of service. Just as good husbands and wives anywhere get through the vicissitudes of life as a team, the best Navy spouses serve their partners and their country as teammates.

An important consideration for current military couples is the way and manner in which you communicate when the Navy orders cause a separation. On my early deployments, I handed the checkbook to my wife the day before departing, and took it back as I walked off the ship's brow at the deployment's end. We shared handwritten letters that were numbered, to ensure they were read in the intended order and not as scrambled by the long-distance mail carriers. We spoke only when there was a landline available in the various foreign ports. Looking back, this was hard! And now the communications and connectivity (for very good and maybe not-so-good reasons) are readily available to those on the front line and those on the home front. When deployed, be especially careful of what you say—for the sake of security and for the health of your relationship.

When it was time for me to retire (after thirty years), it was interesting to see that my associates and our family friends were more concerned about my wife staying in the local area than about knowing what the next step was to be in my second career. The point was accentuated that my wife did make an important difference in my career and the lives of many others in the local and Navy family.

The final takeaway is that your family is important, and within the challenging routines of naval service, you and your command need to carefully balance the needs of the Navy and the needs and preferences of your family. Work-life balance and the desire to focus on a family continue to be primary reasons for officers and enlisted to leave the service.[5]

Navy spouses have a long-held reputation for being spunky, tough, caring, positive, and loyal to both their spouses and the Navy as an institution. When you meet a career officer who has been married for a significant portion (or all!) of their career, you are almost sure to meet a spouse with the wisdom and grace that only comes with the challenges of Navy life. They just might have the hardest job in the Navy! When you attend a retirement ceremony and hear the service member tearfully address and thank their spouse, parents, and children, you can appreciate the importance and impact the family has on giving meaning and joy to a military career.

17

ASSIGNMENT AND PLACEMENT OFFICERS

All detailing is local.

—Cdr. Clay Harris, USN

When I was growing up in the Navy, the personnel office was called BUPERS (Bureau of Personnel) and was located in the Pentagon Annex (now part of Arlington National Cemetery). Before that it was called the Bureau of Navigation—an appropriate name for an organization whose duties included the job of processing officers from assignment to assignment. Today, although there is still a chief of naval personnel, the assignment and placement of officers are done by the Navy Personnel Command in Millington, Tennessee, overseen by the deputy chief of naval personnel.[1] The assignment and placement (slating) of flag officers, however, are still done in Washington.

In my early officer tours, I voiced an interest in being a Navy detailer. I watched and listened to how my XOs and DHs communicated with the "Bureau" on behalf of the crew and for their personal follow-on tours. It was fascinating to me that such a large organization could continue to keep the fleet afloat while ordering the right people into the right positions on eighteen-month or two-year officer rotations. I thought I might have the personality and aptitude to work well in such a position. As a Navy captain, I got my wish and was assigned as the senior detailer and community manager for the engineering duty officer community. Managing the careers of only about six hundred officers was enough and gave me a full appreciation for the challenging efforts of the much larger unrestricted line communities. This chapter does not give you the full detailing "cookbook," but hopefully you get an appreciation for what goes on in BUPERS, and where the focus is to give you the best opportunity to be promoted and meet your career goals.

The Mechanics

The name, location, and technical support of the business have changed over the years, but the heart of the business has not. Despite gossip to the contrary, the detailers still represent you and, with few exceptions, do their best to help you navigate through a succession of assignments that represent a balance between what you want to do, what you should do, and what they (and you) must do. Opposite your detailer or assignment officer stands the placement officer, who represents the commands of the Navy—ships, squadrons, staffs, joint commands, and shore activities, including the various schoolhouses. The placement officer representing the command knows that one of the officers in that command is coming up for rotation. He or she identifies a billet to be filled and a date to fill it. Sometimes the billets are coded for a specific warfare community (for example, surface warfare, subs, aviation, etc.), and sometimes they are generic billets for a certain rank that any community might fill. The community-specified billets are assigned to the appropriate detailer desk to be included in an upcoming slate, with the timing such that a relief will arrive before the incumbent's departure. If it is not community-specific, the billet will be assigned to a community based on a level-loading approach to ensure that each community supports such billets in proportion to its size and margins. The detailers (called assignment officers in other services and monitors in the Marines) receive the newly assigned billet and go over the list of officers for whom they are responsible to see whether there is a match for a qualified officer (perhaps you) becoming available during that time period.

The match should meet the following criteria: the soon-to-be vacant billet fits with your natural career progression, the timing window works, the proposed assignment is consistent with your preferences (if possible), and your performance record is strong enough to warrant such an assignment. In short, once the detailer is satisfied that you are qualified and available for the billet, that officer markets you to the placement officer.

The placement officer tries to avoid gapping the billet and wants you to have the necessary schools and training prior to arriving to your job. The better your performance record, the easier it is for the assignment officer to market you to the placement officer. Occasionally, the receiving command will accept a gap if it means getting a better-suited or higher-quality officer assigned. The tricky part of this process is that no one has an absolute veto—not the assignment officer, not the placement officer, and not you. It is a negotiating process in which the leverage of any given player is limited, but in today's Navy a much greater effort is made to satisfy your preferences when possible. If you are given a choice and you are not interested in an assignment that is career-enhancing (in the detailer's view), you may have to accept a lesser assignment but one that is more in line with your preferences. At the end of the day, the detailer must fill the soon-to-be-vacant billet or persuade the placement officer and the affected command to accept a gap.

One detailer indicates the pitfalls this way:

> An officer who fails to screen or promote will often claim after the fact that a low-impact, fur-lined job may have tipped the scales against him at Board Time. What I have learned is that in most cases, the officer himself went to great lengths to secure that job and took it against his detailer's advice—in some cases with the full blessing and support of his mentor/advisor/sea daddy. What officers may not be aware of is that detailers keep brief electronic records of significant conversations (and e-mail exchanges) with their constituents using screen notes. These notes never go away, unless the detailer erases them. Quite often an assignment officer can look back a few years and find evidence that Lieutenant Commander Smith knew he was taking an assignment against the advice of his then-detailer, that the job would likely be perceived as detrimental to his upward mobility.[2]

Within the negotiation of your career, it is best to ensure that your desires are communicated, clearly and often. An electronic sea slate preference sheet (maintained by the detailers) has replaced the handwritten duty preference card and is your tool to record personal data relevant to your assignments and preference and priority of future assignments. Within the surface warfare officer community, this sheet includes qualifications and your preferences to type of platform, home port, and billet. The (electronic) input from your commanding officer gives the detailers additional insight on your availability and fit for the proposed position. When you see that your projected rotation date is a year out, it is time to start the conversations and be the "squeaky wheel" that gets the necessary attention for consideration of your next set of orders.

Assignment and Placement Officers

The arithmetic of the detailing process is such that there are always more billets than officers available to fill them. The reasons for this are complex but are rooted in the fact that pipelines are always longer than the budgeted number of bodies. People represent money, and Congress grants money on the basis of its perception of what the officer strength of the Navy and the efficiency of its assignment process should be. But as I have indicated throughout this book, some billets are less desirable than others but are still important enough for some officers to be ordered to fill them. A numbers game soon transforms into a quality (of performance) game, a clout game (some commanders bring more leverage to the assignment process), and a game involving your willingness to trade off one preference (for example, a step up the command preparation pyramid) for another (your desire for a particular location). Throughout this process, an emphasis is placed on filling sea billets at the expense of shore billets.

All this is a brokering process whose object is to fill as many billets with as many qualified officers who are satisfied with their assignments as possible. It is not an easy business, and the detailers are at the pointed end of a difficult process. Some call them "flesh peddlers" because they are indeed marketers—selling the placement officers on your fitness for the jobs on offer and selling you on the benefits of the job for your career or in meeting your other preferences. And they have a full set of sales pitches to smooth the process. The following suggests what you might hear.

"We need your expertise in the job."

In this pitch, the detailer emphasizes your experience in a similar job and the need for it in a follow-on job. In this formulation, you are a pro whose abilities are badly needed in the open billet. On the other hand, if you have never been in a similar assignment before, the detailer may pitch it by saying, "You need to broaden your area of expertise to become promotable or more assignable downstream." Early in my career, when steam engineering (and engineering in general) was problematic in the surface warfare community and the Navy was moving to gas turbine propulsion, both these arguments were in place. Successful engineers were recruited to take additional DH tours in steam engineering, and aspiring officers without engineering experience were highly encouraged to take on the gas turbine engineering positions, to understand the Navy's new propulsion and demonstrate their ability to perform in the hard job. Both pitches are legitimate and even honest, but you have to decide whether you want to buy the argument and what you can do about it if it is not what you want.

"This job requires a high-performing officer."
This pitch is not only to your ego but also to get you into a billet (the good hard job) that demands a high performer. The detailer is telling you that the placement officer will not accept just anybody to fill the open billet. The implication is that the billet is a plus in your career planning. But the detailer may also be telling you that you may be put in with a group of highly motivated individuals where the competition will be fierce (which is not all bad).

"This job calls for an officer in the grade of
[the next highest rank]."
This pitch means that the low control grade inventory of officers has shifted priorities and it is better to have a higher performer of a lower rank fill the position rather than leave the billet gapped. Therefore, the system has downshifted to fill it. This can be an opportunity, but it is just as likely that the billet has been misgraded. Another possibility is that the receiving command would rather

have a more junior but higher quality officer (you) than another more senior but less competitive officer offered by the detailers. You have to ask yourself whether serving in the billet on offer would be career-enhancing.

"You were recommended (or you asked) to fill this billet."
This sales pitch is another appeal to your ego. Being asked for is nice, but is this a job that fits in with your progression to screening for command? How will it look to a promotion board? The people who asked for you or recommended you will not be identifiable to or known by the boards—unless the billet is a high-visibility one (in which case there is no problem). A variant of this pitch is that you are among two or three nominees for the job—and the nominees are well known to you to be high performers.

"Your timing is great."
In this pitch, the detailer knows you are coming up before a screening or promotion board (say, in the next year) and that the job on offer will enhance your résumé. In a variation of this pitch, the detailer will say that the boss is well known and that it would be in your interest to have a fitness report signed by that individual before the board meets. Another variation is that you will get to the command just before it deploys and hence will get valuable experience and a chance for a more impressive fitness report. There are many other variations of this game. It is like timing the stock market to buy or sell. You can get stung badly if you are wrong in the face of a fickle future. Remember: job first, timing second.

"You need more operational experience."
This statement may be true, but some operational experiences are better than others. To go to sea and be put on a deployable staff is

helpful in one way, but if it delays assignment to a department head or command track billet, it is not as good as a ship or squadron billet.

"You have been selected for postgraduate instruction."

This may be just what you want. To be selected (meaning you made the cut) and to have an opportunity to earn a degree and to have some shore duty after an arduous sea tour can sound great. But be careful; is that what you really want to do? Getting a fully funded postgraduate degree will result in additional commitments, so for the junior officer, you need to be confident that you want to stay in to complete that commitment and conduct payback tours. For the post-DH or XO, you need to be sure this fits with your follow-on assignments. Some communities have postgraduate education as part of their normal career path, but others do not. For some communities, going to a postgraduate program might be considered "off track" because they are not operational, and you will likely receive a "not observed" FITREP. For many, the benefits of achieving a postgraduate degree outweigh these concerns, but every community is different. Also, some programs are better and more competitive than others, so you need to understand all of the possible ramifications before accepting these orders.

"We need you back ashore."

Whether you think so or not, others think you have been at sea or in command long enough and that it is time to give others a chance. Never be talked into leaving a sea command early, no matter who wants you. You should leave command kicking and screaming. A year in command simply is not long enough to learn the business. Two years is both better and a minimum, in my view. If your shortened tour contained an overseas deployment, you can rest somewhat easier. But the threat of being ripped out just before a deployment should send you to battle stations. Early detachments are normally the result of high-level attention in Navy Personnel Command or in the office of the Chief of Naval Operations. Your presence is demanded now, and there may be little that you can do about it. The detailer may head you off by telling you, "Do not fight these orders because the folks who decide these matters have already decided." But before rolling over, check with the officer who is demanding you to see whether that was the intention—or that you are being rolled. Sometimes you will be ripped out to relieve an officer who has received a high-priority assignment. You are at the end of a daisy chain.

"This is a joint [or combined] billet."
Here the detailer will point out, if you do not already know it, that joint or combined duty is a prerequisite for selection to flag rank.[3] But the type of billet (is it with the J-3 in the Joint Staff or in a small joint technical field activity?) and the timing (should you be at sea at this point?) are important factors. Keep your eye on your objective: qualifying for command at sea. Your flag hurdles should take second in priority behind getting ready for command.

"We need you in the production pipeline."
This will be a comment generally proposed to an aviation junior officer looking at their first short tour. The fleet replacement squadron (FRS) or weapons school is really the priority for the detailers and the aviation community. This ploy is normally used with aviators who are to be ordered to aviation billets ashore. The tour you seek may be good for personal reasons, develop program management or leadership skills, or provide joint experience—but in the end, a Navy aviator is most needed for their technical skills and

expertise in flying. Some shore tours, including the Naval Academy, provide some additional opportunity to maintain proficiency, but the assignments at the FRS or weapons schools provide the daily assignment to fly, train, and build up a logbook of flight hours. Having said this, be assured that the number of flight hours or carrier traps is counted and carries some weight in the ready room, but the number of hours is not part of the assessment that will get you promoted or assigned to the next hard job. As stated throughout, it is not enough to get to good billets; you must perform well while there.

"You are going as an aide to the admiral."
Many years ago, flag lieutenants were designated as staff communicators. These days, flag lieutenants (at sea) and aides (ashore) are more the personal assistants than key members of the staff. They are seldom involved with the substance of the staff's business. Rarely would an admiral ask an aide's opinion on a major matter of substance in making a decision. Aide jobs can be good jobs, but not for the reasons you may think. You may think that you can do no wrong to be working directly for an admiral. You may think that the admiral may be able to help you with getting a plum follow-on assignment. This is wrong thinking, however. An aide's job is good to the degree that you get a broader appreciation of what the Navy is about. You see the decisions your admiral is called on to make. You begin to realize that the Navy is more than your chain of command. You probably will gain some social polish. But the content of most aide jobs is more menial than that. These jobs involve scheduling, travel arrangements, honors, office management, and so on. You will find yourself a mess caterer, a valet, and a fixer, not a key adviser at the right hand of someone at the top. However, in these positions you get to see and be seen, meaning you do get an

appreciation on how your community leadership operates, and you add to your very important professional network.

For the aide, your admiral almost surely will be long retired before that individual would have influence (if any) for the critical milestones for your career. As an executive assistant, however, you will be much closer to the communications and decision process and may be asked to "hold down the fort" while your boss is on travel. This is the time to clearly understand the personality and priorities of your boss, and to not overstep your responsibilities or authorities. "Looping" for a flag officer is a unique opportunity, and my advice is to go into these tours with your eyes wide open.[4] Filling the job does not mean you are one of the anointed; it is an interesting detour as you prepare yourself for command. If you have any control in the matter, do not stay in the job long. In a year you can learn most of what there is to learn.

"There are a lot of perks with the job."
In days past, a captain stationed in command overseas might have a number of perks: a personal auto and driver, special allowances, government quarters, household help—and even a personal aircraft and crew in some overseas assignments. Today the perks are more modest and, in most cases, limited to a few overseas jobs or commanding officer positions. In my experience, the detailer using this claim was trying hard to fill a position that was far off the nominal career path or main highway. When visiting the naval (surface, submarine, and aviation) warfare centers that are far from the coasts, you will be introduced to amazing scenery and phenomenal outdoor recreational opportunities. Although enjoying the environment is good for the soul, the reality is, unless you make the concerted effort to remain in touch and relevant, you can be neglected in consideration for the next good position. The perks

of a good hard job are the personal satisfaction of a job well done and consideration for the next good hard job. It is axiomatic today that a good career job entails long hours, family separation, some personal danger, and a great deal of workplace pressure, or all of the above, to produce.

"This is a new (and important?) billet."
Billets are being established and disestablished daily. Just because the billet is new does not mean it is on the career main line. Many such billets are highly specialized, and their importance may be fad-related. The Navy has fads like any large organization. Special program billets can be very trendy and tricky, so beware.

The Placement Officer

The other half of the assignment equation is the placement officer. You will not have much to do with placement officers until you become an XO or a staff personnel officer. As indicated earlier, placement officers are the command's window into the personnel assignment world. The placement officer's job is to fill the client command's billets with qualified relief and no gaps. If time permits, the placement officer will confer with the command before accepting candidates for their billets. Because some officer types are in short supply (e.g., post-command commanders), some billets will be gapped, filled with more junior (or in some cases more senior) officers or with officers without the necessary credentials of education, warfare qualifications, and so on.

Before one places too many demands on placement officers, remember that by definition, almost half the Navy's officers are below the service-wide performance average (and half are above). This does not mean that such officers cannot do the job—just that they are not recorded as the hottest runners, and in most cases, they need not be to do a good job. It is natural to want the best for your command, but wisdom may lie in the recognition that the best is not always necessary. Indeed, they may cause the command a problem both at fitness report time and in keeping the peace in the wardroom, ready room, or flag mess. You want the best officers for only the very best jobs.

Misconceptions About the Officer Personnel System

There is a widespread perception that favoritism pervades the Navy's personnel assignment and placement systems. This perception is fostered by the fact that some officers do not get the assignments they want and believe they deserve and that somebody else got the desired job because of personal connections. The systems are run by human beings, and they deal in a human product. It is not surprising that misperceptions and disappointments occur. Some very senior officers do attempt to manipulate the system—for example, with a call to the detailer or placement officer's boss or his boss. Some senior officers get their way. And this is not always bad. Any personnel system should strive to be fair, but it should also be responsive to the needs of top management.

What keeps the system fair? First, the detailers have available to them your official records, your duty preference sheets, and a numerical readout on how you stack up with your contemporaries. Although the gradations may be fine and arguable at the margin, detailers will have a good idea as to how competitive you are and whether you are in the hunt for command screening and promotion. If you have screened, they will know your ranking in the screening. But more important than that is the fact that the receiving commands want the best, and it is not to their advantage to accept less than the best when the best are available. If you have an excellent record, you will get a good job because it is in the self-interest of the system and its players to get you into one.

Does it happen that sometimes a less-than-stellar officer gets the best job? It does occur, but not very often. Senior officers, in picking an executive assistant, are sometimes willing to accept less than the best (though few will admit it) in order to get someone they know in the billet that involves daily personal contact. Four-star officers, as senior members of the Navy's board of directors, get considerable latitude in picking their key staff members. And I believe the system is as fair as human ingenuity can make it. This explanation will not satisfy the disappointed candidates who were not selected. But they and their supporters err in my view when they transform personal disappointments into a judgment of systemic weakness.

Dealing with Your Detailer

Keep your relationship with the detailer professional. Detailers have a job to do, and you do, too. Do not be afraid to ask them how you stack up, whether the prospective assignment fills your career needs, what the alternatives are, what negotiating room there is on timing, what schools can be attended en route and, under ideal circumstances, what your follow-on assignment should be. They should also be apprised of any special circumstances in your assignment (e.g., an exceptional family member, a working or military spouse, an impending divorce, or major illness). A detailer may never be your friend but can and should be your professional adviser; strive to keep the relationship from being adversarial. You may respond that it is not your job to solve their problems, particularly if solving them is at your professional expense. This is true, but there is room for courtesy and negotiation, gently pushing the envelope, understanding the give-and-take of the process, and working toward an acceptable if not optimal solution. Not being adversarial, however, does not mean that you should never challenge what the detailer tells you. Orders are orders, but you are also your own advocate and should make sure the detailer fully understands your perspective on the impact of or concerns you have regarding an upcoming assignment.

Some very senior officers I know are proud of the fact that they never challenged a proposed assignment. The assignments ended up challenging them. Because they were very successful, they tended to go to the top jobs anyway. But if you are frequently in the position of having to challenge the detailer's judgment or candor, you should start to ask yourself whether you stack up in professional performance. The best officers do not have to argue for the top assignments. Those who are a step below them and are striving for the top rung are the ones who have the most difficult road. It all goes back to your performance—which is where this book started. This is not to say that a healthy skepticism is not warranted—only to say that the system does pretty well without a lot of self-interested tinkering.

Your assignment dilemmas will include the following:

1. Whether or when to attend a war college or a postgraduate course of instruction. The latter in particular can have a profound effect on your career.
2. Whether to take a somewhat cushy billet that fits in with your family and life objectives or elect to follow a path that might instead include deployments, family separation, home ports with substandard public schools, and so forth.
3. Whether to jump from one warfare or subspecialty track to another.
4. Where and what billet to go to on shore duty.

5. Determining when a projected assignment or your failure to screen is so unacceptable (in your eyes) that you consider resignation or retirement.
6. Whether to extend your tour in any given billet (for the sake of the command mission or for a competitive FITREP).
7. Whether to feather your nest for a future retirement (billets or education that enhance your résumé) or stay in the screening and promotion races.

One of the principal purposes of this book is to give you the necessary background to answer these questions. But such information and advice are useless unless you deal honestly with yourself in appraising your capabilities and shortcomings. When all is said and done, I would hope that you could say you "detailed yourself" through your Navy career. You didn't write or issue the orders, but you were never surprised and you always knew the options available and the advantages and risks associated with the current and next tour. Well before I became a detailer, I was very familiar with the community needs, my potential trajectory, and the detailing process. While the immediate focus was to do the current job well, there was always the discussion with my family, my mentor, and the detailer as to what the next good hard job might be.

As the senior detailer for the engineering duty officer community, I was part of the dance (a better visual than making sausage). And while I was managing the community, I was preparing for the Bureau of Naval Personnel transition from Washington, D.C., to Millington, Tennessee. What I fully appreciated was the positive professional effort of the officers and civilian staff in the Navy Personnel Command to make every effort to meet all the Navy needs and keep everyone happy—to ensure the round pegs got to the round holes, the square pegs to the square holes, while making sure the critical holes were not left unfilled, and moving all the pieces within a carefully monitored travel budget. Considering the metaphorical bureau dance: it is not a ballet, nor is it breakdancing—it is more like a slow waltz where you partner with your detailer to carefully and thoughtfully plan your career.

As I best remember, as the detailer, on only one occasion did I have to say: "You aren't listening—these are orders!" The majority of feedback was: "Thank you for the heads-up, the advice, the status, the consideration, the notification." Work with your detailer and have your eyes wide open considering all there is to a successful Navy career.

Closing Thoughts

- If your boss has a future plan for you—you are tracking.
- If your boss tells you what you need to do next—you are tracking.
- If your boss asks what you want to do next, they are coaching more than mentoring and are searching to understand your career intentions. Think of Navy detailing as an executive training track.
- We need you to have the ability and experience to be an executive leader in the Navy.

Your current tour should not be solely a means to an end. If you do look at it that way, you won't enjoy it; if you don't enjoy it, you won't perform well.

18

THE FITNESS REPORT SYSTEM

Carry out every assignment to the best of your ability. There is no better or faster way to "break out of the pack" than to establish a reputation for reliable and timely performance.

—Rafael C. Benitez, *Anchors: Ethical and Practical Maxims*

To this point, there should be no doubt that your fitness reports are the necessary record of your Navy performance and the one document that will, and must be, reviewed at selection and promotion boards. This chapter kicks off our discussion of the mechanics of promotion and presents principles to consider in the evaluation process, not how you would like to have your boss fill in the boxes on the current FITREP form. That said, we will use current fitness report directives as a backdrop and reference for our narrative.

From the BUPERS Instruction 1610.10F, *Navy Performance Evaluation System*: "Evaluations are the primary source of information for officers and enlisted personnel management decisions and guide member's performance and development, enhance accomplishment of the organization mission, and provide additional information to the chain of command."[1] As Rear Admiral Winnefeld noted in the original edition of this text, "A fitness report is neither a reward nor a form of punishment; it is a tool designed to capture as succinctly as possible that officer's potential for further

The Fitness Report System

service and to convey to an anonymous selection board what that officer is capable of doing for the Navy."

Because of the importance of the evaluation system, the BUPERS instruction is detailed and lengthy, providing guidance for commanding officers, reporting seniors, and raters, and a manual of instruction for completing officer FITREPS and enlisted evaluations. It behooves each officer to be familiar with the complete instruction to understand and know how to prepare for and interpret your personal evaluation and how to prepare and draft the evaluations of your enlisted subordinates.

The detailer shops have produced "FITREP 101" guides to help officers better manage their own records, especially when boards are concerned: "Your FITREP is not a counseling tool. It is a report of your fitness in your current job and an assessment of your ability to succeed at the next level. Specific feedback on your job performance is provided through several other means. Some other facts:

1. If it's not in your record, it didn't happen,
2. Maintain copies of your FITREPs,
3. Review your record before every board, and
4. Are you recommended for the next rank and milestone?[2]

Concerning the Navy's evaluation system, there are three things you can be certain of as your career progresses: the format of the fitness report will change, some form of comparison or distribution of officers of similar rank and career path will be required, and COs will hate to be forced to choose between two or more good officers at fitness report time.

In his weekly radio program, *A Prairie Home Companion*, Garrison Keillor presented the news from Lake Wobegon, "where all the women are strong, all the men are good-looking, and all the children are above average." This has a familiar ring, as in my early years in the Navy, we would ask, "How can 95 percent of the officers be ranked in the top 5 percent?" Without the member trait average, summary group average, or limits on early promote recommendations (which are now in place), COs felt compelled to give everyone high scores, and any breakout or recommendation was restricted to the small box labeled "comments on performance." The changes in the evaluation manual do not make the CO's job easier, but they do give more clarity to a reviewer as to the CO's recommendation and relative standing of the officers evaluated.

In its fundamentals, a fitness report is in five parts: duties assigned, command employment and command achievements, performance traits (e.g., leadership and tactical performance), comments on performance (a narrative), and promotion recommendations. The last three parts are the most important because those are the areas where the reporting seniors do their heavy lifting. Under recent changes to fitness report directives, explicit comparisons and breakouts ("number one of five department heads," for example) are permitted and expected. Reporting seniors who do not break out their players on the back of the report place them at risk. This "promotion recommendations" part of the fitness report format and associated instructions have been the object of a great deal of tinkering over the years.

Timing of Fitness Reports

There are four types of regular fitness reports: periodic reports once a year, reports upon detachment of your reporting senior, reports upon your detachment from the command, and special reports intended to cover a variety of narrowly defined unusual circumstances. Since directives in 1996, officers are to be counseled on their performance midway through the regular report interval so that they have time to remedy any defects in performance before the actual report is prepared. They are again counseled just before the report is sent to the Navy Personnel Command for recording, and the officer reported upon is required to sign the report. Most seniors do not write up shortcomings unless they are gross. Less egregious shortcomings are reserved for the oral counseling. Nothing in a report should be a surprise if the reporting senior has exercised the degree of leadership the Navy expects of that individual.

Narrative Comments on Performance

The FITREP grading system has moved from a percentage standing to a 1–5 evaluation in the critical performance traits. A rating of 5.0 is the "Superstar Performance—could be promoted two paygrades, and still be a standout in this trait," down to a rating of 1.0, "Disappointing Performance—Until deficiencies are remedied, in this trait, should not be promoted, regardless of performance in other traits." And while the scoring and the record of summary group average present a clearer picture of the CO's opinions, the narrative provides the greater insight and impact.

Long fitness report narratives are not desired. The narrative is intended to back up with concrete facts and examples the grading contained elsewhere in the report. This section gives the specifics that cannot be described by checking the boxes in the report. Many COs use the narrative as an opportunity to converse with future screening and selection boards, and that conversation should be terse and to the point. Some skippers use the narrative to reduce the sting administered elsewhere in the report where tough choices have to be made. Most COs make the narrative a combination art form and sales pitch. They are very sensitive to the fact that they are talking to three audiences simultaneously: the Navy Personnel

Command that is in charge of quality control for the fitness report system, future selection and screening boards, and the officer being reported on. Each audience is looking for something different: that the reporting rules are being observed, that the CO is being candid and forthcoming with future board members, and that the officer being reported on (you) is being treated fairly with a proper balance between your strengths and shortcomings, if any.

The quality control authorities have a number of prohibitions to rein in the overly enthusiastic commanding officer. But the most important weapons in the quality control locker are the quota controls on the award of "early promote" and "must promote" recommendations in each group of reports on officers in specific "officer competitive categories," and the comparison of the trait mark average on your report with the summary group average (your competition in the command) required by the fitness report form.

The current system is based on four pillars:

1. Ranking of an officer is compared across promotion recommendation categories (that is, early promote, must promote, promotable, progressing, and significant problems).
2. A system of constraints and incentives for reporting officers wherein grade inflation is kept under some control (for example, numerical limits on top promotion recommendation numbers, or assigning a grade to raters based on the aggregate of their rating distributions).
3. A concerted effort to make performance reporting an integrated and consistent system (for example, greater precision in report formats, more specific instructions for compliance, quality control mechanisms).
4. Counseling is built into the system from the outset. The system is more than a performance recording system; it has mechanisms to encourage awareness of shortcomings and to provide incentives

for improvement. The instruction requires the supervisor's preparation to include engaging with and reviewing the subordinate's self-appraisal to dive deeper and provide specific comments on any areas for development or improvement.

Worthwhile advice for completing the narrative block is included in the manual, including some basic do's and don'ts and recommendations for style and content.

You may ask what all this means for you. It means that you have a good chance of being treated fairly, knowing where you must improve, gauging your promotability, removing some of the previous mystery associated with the process, and having the certainty of face-to-face counseling with your supervisors. Commanding officers must make difficult choices openly and are denied the opportunity of gaming the system. Moreover, grading by commanding officers is the subject of greater institutional scrutiny because the raters' grading tendencies are made more visible. Board members have to work harder than in the old days. The narratives must be read more closely to assess performance differences among officers in the same promotion category. On the other hand, board members have more tools available with a more precise fitness report format and the means to better understand how given commanding officers are rating their officers (by comparing individual and command-wide trait averages). Now let us turn to how the fitness reports and the various reports that summarize them are used by the boards and assignment officers.

Boards Read the Tea Leaves

As stated, periodic efforts are (and will be) made to "reform" the system. In part, these efforts are the result of frustration by screening and selection boards as they attempt to filter out the extraneous, the trivial, the routine, and the puffery put in the reports by some commanding officers. In too many cases, board members must take on the role of detectives, trying to ascertain what your reporting senior really meant. A tension exists between the roles of reporting seniors and board members. Commanding officers want to keep their wardroom morale high by giving good (or better) fitness reports as they urge officers on to top performance. Because they counsel their officers and because these officers see their fitness reports, seniors feel an obligation to be both candid and laudatory. The natural tendency is to overdo praise and soften criticism. Unfortunately, this practice tends to lull some average or below-average officers into an unwarranted sense of security.

The screening and promotion boards have to sift through all the words, markings, and rankings and pick the very best. Typical commanding officers and their fitness reports make the boards' job very difficult, and, unfortunately, some boards do not always get it right. Some commanding officers believe more is better than less when it comes to writing a fitness report, a practice that puts additional obstacles in the way of understanding. These facts of life have forced boards to rely heavily on comparative rankings—where the writer-skipper must finally declare who is the best or among the best, next best, and so on. But COs do not give up easily and do their best to avoid being put in a corner.

What You Want the Fitness Report to Say

You want your fitness report to say the following:

1. You held a demanding job and did so for a protracted period. Past a junior officer tour, your orders will most likely determine the

position you will have within the command. In particular, some DH jobs are recognized as harder than others, and the CO needs to evaluate your performance in the assignment you've been given, to keep every officer qualified and competitive when that individual's record appears before the XO and CO screening boards.
2. You did so while deployed. You were tested in a demanding environment, and the fitness report narrative states the salient details of the deployment and your role in it.
3. You performed well compared to your contemporaries in similarly demanding jobs. A mark in the "must promote" box is acceptable until you can further prove you have the right stuff to make the "early promote" box. Time on board can often give the nod to the officer with more time in the job.
4. The narrative supports with facts the quality of your accomplishments. This is a must!
5. You are qualified for the next step in your career progression, such as department head, executive officer, commanding officer, or major command.

Although your fitness report principally documents your past performance, it should also forecast your future promise. You perform well not only for the satisfaction of doing a good job but also because that performance is a partial predictor of your future performance in positions of higher responsibility. Your fitness report is intended to speak to future screening and promotion boards, not the historical researcher or the record keeper. The whole report must be forward looking, using past performance as one indicator. The other indicators are your intellectual capacity, your suppleness of mind, your ability to learn from experience and observation, and your suitability for professional growth. As important as these other indicators are, they are crucially affected by proven performance.

Fashioning this linkage between the past and the future is the job of the screening and promotion boards. They can do no better than the raw materials they must work with, meaning principally your reports of fitness. Remember that the members of the boards who judge your suitability have been where you want to go. They know what it takes, and they are looking for what you have to offer that fits the requirement template. In a sense, your former COs are their guides in making this assessment.

Danger Signals in Your Fitness Report

You will have an opportunity to read your fitness report and ask your CO questions about it. The best-prepared COs will provide you a copy of your FITREP early, so you can come to your meeting having read it and being ready to talk about it. This does not always happen, though. Look especially for qualifiers that sound good but on closer examination pull the punch on an evaluation. Such qualifiers include: "One of the best officers in this command," "Usually performs well," "Can be depended on," and "Does assigned tasks well."

Another danger signal is a lack of specificity in the report. The use of general descriptors suggests that your skipper either does not know you (and consequently your performance) very well and is padding the report or is feeding the board (and you) pablum that says pass on a pass/fail test but does not tell you why (or whether) you are better than your running mates. Some commanding officers use general descriptors of praise as a substitute for criticism. A variant of the general (and not very useful) descriptor is the presentation of irrelevant material: "He likes his job" (so what?). "She works hard." "He boosts wardroom morale" (life of the party? See chapter 6). "She has a sense of humor" (how does that help the command and her performance?). "He is a good administrator" (also a good operator and maintainer?).

Sometimes there will be veiled criticism in the fitness report: "He reacts positively to suggestions." "He learns quickly with experience." "He has lost weight and is now in good physical condition." "With his current upward trend in performance I believe he will soon be a superb performer." Comments of this type should prompt a discussion with your executive officer or commanding officer to get specifics and to find out in concrete terms what more they expect of you or where you have not met their standards. Ideally, of course, you will already know why those comments are in the FITREP, because you and your chain of command should have covered your performance and possible areas of improvement during midterm counseling.

Some closing thoughts on the block 41, comments and performance (narrative), section of your FITREP. It cannot be overstated how important the message is that is delivered in this relatively small space. Attachments are not routinely accepted or expected. So, make the time to carefully address the most relevant and persuasive elements of your performance. There are numerous websites and blogs on which prior military readily provide hints on phrases and terms that they have found to be helpful or hurtful. Some of their advice might be helpful (or hurtful). Another uncertainly in this area lies in the advancement of generative artificial intelligence. The technology is readily used in drafting résumés, and the probable utilization in crafting FITREPs and evaluations may make the differential of officer and enlisted performance even more difficult. Pay attention to the advancements in this technology!

What Boards Are Looking for in the Fitness Report Narrative

Boards are looking for concrete evidence of achievement, examples that make a point in your favor (or against), and tangible evidence that your performance is superior to that of your peers. Notice the specifics in the exemplar comments that follow.

- "Performed both regular duties and those as acting XO for two months while regular XO hospitalized; maintained effectiveness and morale in the command and in her department."
- "Was first first-tour aviator arriving on this turn-around cycle to become fully weapons qualified. His landing grades were the best for his rank in the squadron."
- "Was most junior officer to become fully qualified officer of the deck (OOD) underway (formation) in command during this reporting period. Executed an effective and safe emergency breakaway from oiler during an actual steering casualty."
- "Although her squadron is not yet best in the air wing, it is the most improved, and she would be my first choice to relieve my deputy CAG if the need arose."
- "Have deliberately loaded him up with a myriad of extra duties beyond his billet and pay grade for the simple reason that under pressure he is the most effective officer in the command and is absolutely dependable. Is the 'go to guy' in the command."
- "Knows more about the installed weapons system than anyone in the command, including her chief petty officers and me. Reduced CASREP [casualty report] rate for systems in her department by half with no change in supply priorities. The one indispensable person serving in this ship."

Your Input to Your Fitness Report

Your commanding officer is required under current directives to obtain your input to your upcoming fitness report. Your input should be in the form of an information sheet that can be used as a basis for documenting your performance. Sometimes this is a simple listing of duties performed, qualifications gained, off-duty education completed, next duty preferences, and so on. But with care you can go beyond that and provide some detail that may at first glance seem trivial to you but will catch your skipper's eye.

Ask yourself what changes you have made in your division or area of responsibility since you took over. If there are tangible and beneficial results to those changes, tell your bosses what they are. Ask yourself what steps you have taken to qualify yourself for your boss's job. This may be as simple as standing in for that officer when absent or taking on a special project for the person, a project that might get lost in the larger overview your bosses have. Have you kept an "attaboy" file or a file that contains all the "Bravo Zulus" (Well done!) you or your shop have received? Fitness report time is the time to trot them out and append them to your data sheet—even if your CO or XO has already seen them. Look over the records kept by your division/shop to see if any data there support uptrends in performance for which you have some responsibility.

You should also be aware that you can do even more to document your performance beyond lists and facts. Append a narrative summary to your fitness report input that weaves the facts together and is crafted in such a way that your senior could, if so inclined, lift sentences and paragraphs out of it for placement in the finished report. You may be doing your senior and yourself a favor—and polishing your writing skills along the way. This is not self-promotion; it is completed staff work, and you should always be your own best advocate. Command- and XO-dependent, this input may look very much like a draft FITREP.

Trends

Some of you will become discouraged because you seem to be in "the pack." That is, your performance as documented in your fitness reports does not show you breaking out to the "must promote" or "early promote" categories. Note, however, that selection and screening boards are intensely interested in trends. For example, if in a two-year tour under two COs you get two "promotable" ratings, followed by a "must promote" rating, followed in turn by an "early promote" rating, I guarantee you will have the full attention of board members. Trends (up or down) are very important. Changes in your promotion recommendation across COs are also important. These changes are even more important when your new and old skippers have a significant variance in their command-wide grade average. The point is that if you are lower than you want to be or think you should be, that should be your first topic in your counseling session with the boss. Catch that updraft! Better yet, make it yourself.

There is a good chance you will get a "farewell bouquet" from your CO when you are detached. It is that person's chance to put you 1 of 1 in the "early promote" category of your detachment report. But if your earlier reports have placed you in the pack, this farewell kudo loses its punch—promotion boards respond most to competitive FITREPs where you are ranked against your peers. Missing the 1 of 1 early promote and anything less than the best marks in your detachment report could send a negative signal to your next selection or screening board. Do not be lulled into a sense of complacency by the glow of a hand-tooled report that is looking only at you and not at the competition.

The Lure of Self-Delusion

In conjunction with the thought just expressed above, never forget that life is a competitive business, whether in the civilian world or in the service. To be "the best" by definition implies ranking and competition. If you selectively listen to and read words of praise but tune out the background, you are setting yourself up for future disappointment. Situational awareness is a prime attribute of successful naval officers. If you are in the pack (as defined by the relevant fitness reports) and stay in the pack over time, at some point you are going to fail to screen or be selected for promotion. All the nice words and reassurances of your friends, mentors, and COs are not going to save you from that disappointment if your fitness reports do not show you breaking out. It is not enough to think, "I have done all they have asked of me." You must do better than that and demonstrate that you are in the front rank of those being screened for command or selected for promotion.

Most failures to screen or be promoted can be traced back to some less-than-above-average performance. The complaints and excuses that define the aftermath of that disappointment can in turn be laid at the doorstep of self-delusion. It is rarely the fault of "the system" if you miss the hurdle, though it is a convenient scapegoat. If you pay attention to the emerging pattern in your fitness reports over time, you will see the first signs of success or disappointment. Your job is to influence the trend if you wish to progress in your naval career. Competing ably and fairly, and having a record that shows this, is the definition of success in the Navy.

Some Administrative Remarks

You do not have to go to Navy Personnel Command to view the most important parts of your promotion jacket or your performance summary report. You can ask for delivery of a disc with the necessary information tailored to your record (ask your detailer where to start), or you can do most of it at your own computer by logging onto BUPERS Online (BOL).[3]

Your responsibility goes beyond reviewing the material received, however. Conceivably, there are gaps in continuity in your fitness report stream. Perhaps a report from your command (old or current) did not find its way to the Navy Personnel Command. Perhaps there is an unintended gap in the continuity of reports. Every day of your career must be accounted for. It is up to you to bring the errors or omissions to the attention of your command, the Navy Personnel Command, or both. BOL is updated every Saturday, and you should make ready access to that account, as you are the first and final quality control officer for your promotion jacket—as to both content and compliance.

19

SCREENING AND PROMOTION BOARDS
And the Verdict Is...

The best news that you will ever receive is that you screened for command.

—Anonymous naval aviator

The mechanics of promotion boards are fairly straightforward. The records of all eligible officers are assembled and reviewed by the boards. Members of the board will be assigned to summarize and brief each record to the entire board.[1] Then, in secret, members will vote electronically. Often a large number of votes is taken until the field is winnowed down to the finalists. The remaining records are again briefed to the board (by different briefers), and votes are again taken until the final and authorized number is selected.

"Promotion boards" are statutory boards whose status and authority are determined by law. They are established and provided guidance under the direction of the Secretary of the Navy, and the boards answer to that individual, not anyone else in the department. The secretary provides guidance letters ("precepts") to the boards that state, among other things, how many officers to select and the skills and characteristics wanted in the selectees. The secretary does not have the authority to tell the board members whom to select. The secretary's authority is to approve or disapprove the board's results or, in rare cases, to strike selectees off the list for a specific reason.

"Screening boards" are administrative boards in that they are ordered by the commander of the Navy Personnel Command. Practices vary, but screening boards are used primarily to select candidates for executive officer and commanding officer. In some cases, even department heads are so selected. Keeping in touch with your detailer on the timing and status of screening boards is important as there may be first, second, and third looks for each of the DH, XO, and CO positions. Screening boards follow most of the same procedures as promotion boards. They have numbers of selectees specified in the convening letter, but they also may have included numbers for specified subcommunities within a warfare community. The screening boards serve as a critical way station on the career track. Faring well before screening boards is just as important as promotion boards in your career progress. Screening boards provide you with a ticket to the game. Promotion boards ratify whether you have done a good job in using that ticket.

Members of promotion boards will be drawn from across warfare communities in proportionate numbers to the entire population. Screening board composition, however, is entirely from your warfare community (for example, aviation, surface warfare, submarine, special warfare). Members of the board will be at least one rank senior to the candidates before the board. The president of the flag promotion board is a four-star officer and is assisted by two or more three-star officers and several two-star officers.

Between summarizing and briefing activities that culminate in the board's voting, there is much discussion among members of the board concerning qualifications of the officers being considered. Some records are so outstanding and the officers' professional reputation so striking that they are selected early in the process. Another group is comprised of officers who have experienced chronic career difficulties and are poor prospects for promotion. In the middle—typically 50 percent or more of the officers examined—the judgments are harder, and the pool receives much closer scrutiny. The "finals" in the deliberative process are a soul-searching exercise for board members. Would I want to have this officer serve under me? What is that officer's skipper really saying? What is left unsaid? What was the competition in that command (sometimes the board finds the answer to that question because the candidate's competitors are often before the same board)? Does this officer show future promise beyond a good record of past performance? Is the officer a candidate to enter the pool of future candidates for flag (in the case of the captain promotion board and major command screening board)? Has this officer taken the easy path, or has the individual been severely tested in areas of high professional risk?

In one key way, promotion boards are different from screening boards. Promotion boards consider not only those officers in the promotion zone but also those in the eligibility zone. An officer in the promotion zone who is not selected in a previous board is considered to have failed of selection ("passed over"), whereas an officer who is merely eligible from below the zone has one or more additional chances before being considered passed over. An officer who is passed over enters special career status. There is always the opportunity for, and there is a history of, officers to be selected "above zone," but a second pass over is usually the person's ticket to civilian life—either retirement or release from active duty.

The Navy's practice on early promotions (selection from below, or junior to the promotion zone) varies from time to time. Under some Navy secretaries and in some circumstances, an emphasis is made on getting new blood by promoting more officers earlier. At other times, the question of seasoning and fairness to those in the zone takes precedence. At any rate, the numbers of officers selected early are small—and the accolades are great for those who achieve it. To be selected early marks you as a standout in your profession and destined for good jobs and high rank if you keep up the level of your performance. Yet it is also a fact of life that many officers who reach flag rank were never selected early for anything. If you are not selected early, you are still very much in the race. If you are selected early, you have been given a major compliment, and much is expected of you. But humility is also called for because you know the race does not always go to the swift.

MyNavy HR provides additional career progression guidance concerning normal promotion flow points, normal selection rates, and instructions for maintaining your officer military personnel file and rules for communicating with a selection board.[2] In December of each year, the CNO publishes Navy administrative messages (NAVADMIN) that announce the convening of upcoming promotion and continuation selection boards for active-duty officers. The junior in-zone eligible and those officers senior to the junior in-zone officer are eligible for promotion in each competitive category. Additionally, the NAVADMIN also specifies below-zone eligible officers, who are the junior eligible officer. Knowing your officer precedence number (a lineal number, assigned to all ensigns) will tell you whether your record will be reviewed at an upcoming board.

Boards are directed to select on the basis of the record (not service reputation). Yet it is impossible not to be influenced by the service reputation of a candidate before the board and of the senior who signed the reports of fitness. Board members are careful not to influence deliberations by personal biases or preferences. But when a board is groping for fuller knowledge about a candidate, a member who can clarify the point will step up and try to clear the air based on personal knowledge. When this is done, caveats and qualified statements are usually used. In my experience and in almost all cases, at least one member of the board knows either the candidate or the senior who signed important reports of fitness. There are few mystery candidates or reporting seniors.

Personal knowledge of a candidate, knowledge that could be considered adverse, cannot be discussed unless the information appears in the eligible member's official record. This guidance is strictly enforced during board proceedings. Additionally, the boards meet in private, and the results of the boards are not to be announced before the secretary or other convening authority acts on the recommendations. No contact is allowed between board members or recorders and persons whose jackets are before the board. The secretary's formatted board announcement states, "Unless expressly authorized or required by the President, Secretary of Defense, or me, no member of the board, recorder, assistant recorder, or administrative support personnel may disclose the proceedings, deliberations, or recommendations of the promotion selection boards."[3] If your boss is going out of town for a temporary duty assignment and isn't more specific of their whereabouts, there is a good chance they are headed to Millington for a board, and they want to avoid any opportunity for an early discussion or influence in their role on the board. Deliberations of the boards are strictly private, and leaks are expressly prohibited.

Most screening boards rank their selectees to help the detailer and placement officers in filling the various slates. Occasionally, officers at the bottom of the list will be "descreened" in a subsequent screening because changed circumstances have made the targeted billets unavailable (for example, unplanned ship retirements). Just because you have screened does not mean you stay screened.

You will be reviewed again the following year if you are not in a billet for which you screened. Some of the most rancorous discussions between senior detailers and screened officers occur when an officer for some reason has experienced descreening. There is the perception of favoritism in spite of the fact that screeners are ranked and that the bottom screeners are the first bumped and get the less-than-most-desirable slots.

Another source of rancor in major command screening is the split between the shore and sea command lists, with the latter being the most desirable. The screening board makes a major effort to ensure balance in quality between the two lists. All the candidates are strong, but some have better seagoing credentials than others do, and the split is up to each board.

One piece of advice here: As you go up the promotion ladder, keep a sharper eye on command screening than on promotion boards. Screening boards are made up of officers from your warfare community, and they know not only the community but also the people (including your skipper) who serve in it. Both a good fitness report jacket and a good service reputation are needed to screen.

If you stay in the Navy long enough, there is a good chance you will be ordered to serve on one of the Navy's many personnel boards: augmentation (into the regular Navy), screening, promotion, decorations and awards, discharge review, aviator disposition, correction of naval records, and so on. It is an important duty, and you will look back on such an assignment with a new respect for the diligence and integrity of those who serve on these boards. Officers are highly encouraged to volunteer to sit on boards as early as they are eligible, not just to gain important board experience, but also because it will typically improve their personal record when they see firsthand what is valued and what isn't in the FITREP writing and record analysis process.

20

ADVICE FOR MIDSHIPMEN

> For in this modern world, the instruments of warfare are not solely for waging war. Far more importantly, they are the means for controlling peace. Naval officers must therefore understand not only how to fight a war, but how to use the tremendous power which they operate to sustain a world of liberty and justice, without unleashing the powerful instruments of destruction and chaos that they have at their command.
> —Adm. Arleigh Burke, August 1, 1961, change of command address at U.S. Naval Academy

This chapter contains some additional career advice for midshipmen and other officer candidates. Some readers will have no intention of making the Navy a career. They want to serve their country, but at an early point in their naval service they plan to return to civilian life. Still, while in service, most want to perform as well as they can and be able to look back on their naval career, however brief. They want their time to be well spent and to learn leadership skills and habits of performance that will stand them well in any future endeavor.

Good advice to all regardless of career intentions is to get into the habit of performing well in any job you are assigned. This keeps all the doors open. We are creatures of habit, and if we try to do well and expect it of ourselves, we will continue to do it regardless of our occupation. Some young officers make a mental reservation that it is not important whether they do well. All they have to do is get by, and then when they return to the "real world," they will take things more seriously. Such thinking is certainly wrong. You need to get into the habit of success; shifting paradigms is not easy, and success is not assured.

It is never too early to work on a good professional reputation and to get into a pattern of success. Naval Academy midshipmen in particular are already embarked on making a service reputation that will see you through a full naval career. Your fellow midshipmen will quickly size you up and will duly note improvements and declines in performance over your four years at the academy. There are seven year groups—three ahead and three behind your class—that will march through a naval career with most of you. Accordingly, for good or ill, you already are gaining a solid basis for a service reputation.

For officers from commissioning sources other than the academy, your service reputation base starts out narrower because you have fewer midshipmen in your NROTC unit or your OCS class. But this disadvantage quickly declines as soon as you enter the fleet, and before too long you have caught up to your academy peers.

As a long-term instructor of midshipmen at the academy, I am regularly asked what it was like in the "real Navy" and to give practical advice they could put to use immediately upon graduation. They do not want long lists of preferred character traits but rather to know how to do it: how to get to the right positions, how to deal with "real Navy" issues, and how to be a success as a junior officer and ultimately become a senior officer in command. What I do remind the midshipmen of is that they are currently in the "real Navy" and their "real" role and "real" responsibility are as midshipmen. They should "well and faithfully discharge the duties" of the office of midshipman, and by diligently following that order, they will be better prepared for the new roles and responsibilities once commissioned.[1]

The additional misconception held by some midshipmen and officer candidates is that things will be very different when they get in the "real Navy." And they cannot wait to get there! Any commissioning program requires rules and regulations designed to make students qualified to receive a commission. Some rules are better than others, but together they compose a complete set. They change over time with circumstances in the service and in society, but to complain about them while you are in the process sets a bad precedent for yourself (complaining is a carryover sport). Once commissioned, it will be different, but leadership will still require subordination to the chain of command and success requires attention to the innumerable fleet rules and regulations, which are not so very different from what they experienced as midshipmen or cadets.

In the original edition of *Career Compass*, Rear Admiral Winnefeld outlined career advice in the form of twelve commandments—applicable (then and now) to all midshipmen or Navy candidates who are looking downstream at the potential of a Navy career.

1. Go where the action is. With regard to service selection, the advice was the Navy equivalent to the Army's "marching to the sound of guns." Try to get to a command that is going to a theater of action. In peacetime, select a ship that will soon be a deployer. Get into the combat forces and not support occupations. This advice was not intended to offend those going into the restricted line or staff corps (some of them go to war, too), but to tell midshipmen that our service is a warfighting one and that success is largely determined by how well you prepare as a warfighter. You cannot always predict

where the theater of action will be, but you can play the odds and go where you think the action will be.

2. Seek to work for the best officers you can find. This is another variable over which you do not have a great deal of control, and as a junior officer you may not have much insight. Nevertheless, you may be surprised to find that even in an era of long training pipelines, you often have some say over what department or subunit you are assigned to—perhaps not right after reporting aboard but later when you get your sea legs. Do not be afraid to work for "hard but fair" leaders. They will teach you the seagoing profession.

3. Prepare yourself for command. If you have read the earlier chapters of this book, you do not need any further elaboration on this point. As a midshipman, accept commanding roles, and as Admiral Nimitz said, "When in command—command."

4. Be the first to get qualified. As a junior officer in any unit, you will face a succession of qualification hurdles—officer of the deck, your dolphins, your surface or aviation warfare pin, your plane commander designation, your engineer of the watch qualification, your department head screening, and so on. All such qualifications take a great deal of study and your personal initiative. The sooner you qualify, the sooner you will be on the watch bill, and the sooner others will see you as a competent and contributing member of the team.

5. Look for opportunities to educate yourself. Your education should not stop when you get your academy or college diploma. Your professional growth will depend greatly on your ability to study on your own, to observe keenly what is going on around you, to mentally "fleet up," and to cultivate what aviators call "situational awareness." Take correspondence courses to keep your intellectual tool locker energized. Be a reader of current events and military history—especially as you deploy to overseas theaters of action.

Advice for Midshipmen

6. Do not rest on your Naval Academy background (or elite college degree). There is a tendency among some midshipmen to believe that their academy background will carry them through their early career and that extra effort is not required. We, as academy staff, work hard to overcome that misconception. This principle applies to whatever your prior background. If you have prior enlisted service and graduate from officer candidate school, you cannot rest on your prior fleet service as giving you a head start for long.
7. Do not worry who gets the credit. You may run into shipmates—perhaps even some bosses—who will take the credit when things go right. Do not worry about it; the people who count will know where the truth lies, and your reputation will be enhanced if you do not jostle for the limelight. Be ready to acknowledge what "we" have done over bringing attention to your personal role.
8. Stay as close to the operating forces as you can. This is still good counsel for junior officers but must be tempered when applied to more senior officers. For example, senior officers cannot afford to spend more time on fleet staffs (even deploying fleet staffs) if they need a responsible job in Washington to round out their career or to prepare for such a job in a prior apprenticeship tour.
9. Keep your sense of humor. A naval career can, and indeed should, be fun. Part of the makeup of most successful officers is a keen sense of humor. This is not the ability to laugh at the foibles of others, but at oneself. A sense of humor adds to your perspective of proportion and balance, makes you a better shipmate, and eases you over the inevitable disappointments of a Navy career.
10. Look out for your people. Look for a division officer or junior division officer billet to get early experience in leading Sailors. You will gain so much looking out for them—but that is only half of the bargain. The other half is that they must measure up to your standards. Too many junior officers construe the first half to mean

blind support for their enlisted personnel at mast, special request chits, and so on, without insisting on their performing at a level that warrants your loyalty. Your job as a leader is to set the terms of the bargain and see that the bargain is kept. Loyalty is a two-way street.[2]

11. You will succeed or fail as a division officer, department head, or CO depending on your relationship with your chief petty officers. Cultivating a positive relationship with them, one that puts the unit first, is your most important job aside from developing personal competence in operating your weapons system.
12. Take all career advice (including this) with a grain of salt. There are many roads to career success, and many think theirs is the only sure one. As a midshipman, make the very most of your summer training and pursue the mentorship of the junior officers who are satisfied with their early career choices. You will receive much advice; take it seriously, but consider it in the context of the speaker's situation and other advice you receive.

There is a necessary addition to the final point. At the very beginning of your commissioned career, there will be a major inflection point where you select or are assigned down a particular career path. Called "service assignment" or, in the case of aviation officer candidate programs, "pipeline selection" (what types of aircraft you will be trained to fly), the decision will determine where your compass needle points. Sometimes the structure of the program, your professional grades in training, or pure luck makes the decision for you. But if you do have a choice, your selection will be extremely important to your future career and how well you do in it. It deserves very careful thought. Too many fledgling officers make the choice for superficial reasons, as a result of peer pressure as to what is considered glamorous, or because assignment to a particular locale appears attractive. Be thoughtful and as informed as possible before making the decision.

One final piece of advice here: In the fleet, you will be serving with officers from many commissioning sources—the Naval Academy, NROTC, OCS, warrant officers, and limited duty officers up from the enlisted ranks. The sharp edges that are so evident to midshipmen and junior officers blur over time, and soon you will not give the commissioning source of your associates a second thought as they become shipmates and friends, colleagues, bosses, and subordinates. You will find that what counts is not a commissioning source but how well the officer performs—whether the individual is a professional. You will also find that you must compete on your own merits and that over the long run, no one has a pedigree advantage over their running mates. You must get that advantage the old-fashioned way: you must earn it.

21

ADVICE FOR THOSE WHO HAVE MISSED A HURDLE

> All advice is opinion.
>
> —Anonymous

What if you were not on the screening or promotion selection list? For most, it is a crushing blow because it is unexpected. You received what you considered were good, solid fitness reports and touched most if not all of the career development bases. You may have had a stumble early in your career but thought you had put it behind you. Or you tried hard to get the really good jobs, but something always seemed to get in the way of a desired assignment. But what really got you were the numbers. Statistically, it is impossible for all good and qualified officers to make the grade of commander and captain, to say nothing of flag. That is not to say your services are not needed. Many important billets need to be filled, and you are qualified to fill many of them. Unfortunately for you, you may not be asked to fill those billets at the more senior grades.

As a community detailer, I would discuss and plan out an officer's career pointing to command and to captain. Anything beyond that was out of our control. And if you make flag, you are not only good, but also lucky. However, there were hurdles along the way to command and O-6, and if you failed selections or promotions along the way, you have a major decision to make. You can take any one of three paths: you can seek billets in the near term that are more personally satisfying and possibly more beneficial to a second career in civilian life, you can seek a billet that may improve your chances of selection the next time around, or you can resign or retire if eligible.

Weighing the Decision to Stay or Go

Almost every promotion board picks some officers from above the promotion zone—that is, from the pool of officers who have been passed over one or more times. Boards stick with this practice even at the price of denying selection to another officer in the promotion zone. There is a widespread conviction that an incentive must be provided for the very best officers previously overlooked for promotion. For the passed-over officer, it is a very difficult decision to stay on the career track for one more turn before the next board. It does not help that keen disappointment clouds one's judgment at such a time. But bear in mind that the next board will be made up of officers who did not serve on your last board.

What should you do? If you believe that you were near the cusp for selection, it could be wise to take another turn before the next board. If you are due for orders, talk to your mentor and detailer and get their advice as to what future assignments might push you over the top. On the other hand, if accepting such an assignment would lock you into a longer tour than you are willing to risk, you should look around for a tour that better fits in with your future plans—perhaps to a location you want or a job experience that would fill out your job search résumé.

Plenty of satisfying jobs are available for officers who have failed of selection. After all, you have the experience; you just lack the rank. Shrewd placement officers and commanding officers of some commands know what a treasure trove the pool of officers who have been passed over is. In that pool are some officers who have held command, many of them successfully. There are officers whose résumé perhaps was unbalanced by too much shore duty but who have just the experience needed for another demanding and satisfying shore tour. With few exceptions, the pool contains officers who would be instantly recalled in the event of war or a major national emergency.

If your mentor is suggesting a new opportunity for a desirable job that may get you to the top of the selection list, you might want to talk to or visit with the incumbent to see if there are aspects that would increase your chances in the next board. But overhanging these options and decisions is the fact that you are getting nearer to having to start your second career. Everyone in the Navy has to think sooner or later about such a career shift. If you are a passed-over officer, that decision is coming sooner, but it was inevitable in any case. You begin to realize that the Navy is a young person's service, and you have to consider when you want to start your second career. Often, but not always, sooner is better than later—particularly if you have family obligations.

Having made the calls to officers (some close friends) who failed to select, I will give some advice here: do not go into autopilot if you get the bad news. Do not head for the door right away—particularly when your disappointment is high. Give the decision to go or stay the same deep thought that you have given each step of your career to this point. Do not too quickly reject the option of giving it another try. You are still a good officer. You still have a good future inside or outside the Navy. The answer is

Advice for Those Who Have Missed a Hurdle

what it has always been from the beginning: a matter of timing and careful decision-making.

Most officers who fail a selection are disappointed but take that disappointment with good grace and a mature acceptance of responsibility for the success of their naval career. But you will also hear some explanations and complaints, and we should examine them. This listing of oft-heard complaints is not intended to mock officers who have been passed over or failed to screen. Rather, it is intended to provide a sampling of warning signals for you to heed as you chart your own career before you are confronted with a career disappointment.

Frequently Heard Explanations

Within the engineering duty officer community, we made every effort to have a flag officer contact the officers affected by a selection board one day prior to the release of the message. This is an acceptable and helpful step to minimize the excitement and/or shock of being on either side of the ledger. But due to random circumstances, I was sometimes the one to call and let officers (in some cases, my good friends) know of their fate before the news was public. In particular, my calls, not a flag call, to officers who did not select gave an open opportunity for venting to me about the system. Here are some responses that are understandable, but still probably not acceptable.

"I was set up to fail." The speaker goes on to say, "I was given an impossible job (or given no support from my seniors), so I was the scapegoat." This lament parallels what I consider one of the most whining paragraphs in modern literature: "More and more it was beginning to appear that he had been asked to do the impossible, but if he failed it would not be remembered that he had been asked to do the impossible. It would only be remembered that he had failed."[1]

In the 1970s, post-Vietnam, when the surface fleet was worn from the years of deferred maintenance, an increasing number of ships were failing propulsion exams. Chief engineers were routinely fired, and their reliefs took one of two positions: this is an opportunity, as the only way from here is up, or this ship is a lost cause, and I am fodder that protects the CO and the maintenance staff. With the number of officers ordered to the chief engineer position without previous engineering experience, the response here was routine and maybe understandable—but not acceptable.

"My skipper had it in for me." When you hear this explanation, your first questions should be: Why was that? What is it about you that ticked that person off? Did the skipper have it in for others, too? Commanding officers did not get to where they are by randomly picking on subordinates. Some subordinates require more attention or supervision than others. Repeated subpar performance calls for increased supervision which in turn can be interpreted as harassment by the poor performer. In extreme cases, a diligent skipper follows Adm. Rafael Benitez's maxim: "If a subordinate repeatedly fails to measure up despite continuous counseling, act decisively. Relieve that person from his or her duties, no matter how painful the experience."[2] Being relieved is a one-way ticket to a failure of selection in almost every case. It should come as no surprise that officers who are relieved usually believe they have been injured unfairly.

Some COs are more patient than others. And some are more decisive than others. Still others work around the problem, and the poor performers soon find themselves ignored and their work being done by others. You try a skipper's patience at your professional peril, and if you find others attempting to do your job, you are receiving an early warning of the need to improve your performance.

"I can't understand why I wasn't selected—I had good jobs and did them well." The target of this claim often starts with a curt call to the detailer and then a questioning discussion with one's mentor. After all, it was the detailing shop that sold the officer on the orders, both in the importance of the position and the probability of positive recognition for doing well. Depending on the prior engagement with one's mentor, the follow-up will probably require a relook at the specifics of the command's outcomes and comparative fitness reports, and how each of those elements led to a reflection on future opportunities. Sadly, there are many very good and challenging positions where there is no peer breakout, and as mentioned before, if the CO is not diligent and careful in the wording of a fitness report, the good hard job will not be recognized by a selection board.

As a senior detailer, having reviewed numerous records before a selection or promotion board, I was often surprised by the outcomes. On those occasions, I was mostly unprepared to provide a satisfactory response to this claim. I was not a member of the board, and I may have even "penciled in" individuals for the next good hard job. My earnest response was that I couldn't change the board's decision but was ready to engage in serious discussions concerning the next steps.

"My skipper was interested only in his own future." The listener should pose the question, "What is this connection with your failure to be selected?" It is easy to confuse an appropriate zeal to meet the command's mission and advance its performance and welfare with the skipper's self-interest. By definition, the CO is the only person with total responsibility for the command. It is true that some COs confuse command performance with personal advancement. Still, to suggest that career is the skipper's primary focus is to attribute base motives to that individual and, by implication, higher motives to the speaker.

In a worst-case situation, that leaves the unanswered question of how the allegation of self-interest is connected to a subordinate's failure to be selected for promotion. Your CO wants to see you promoted if you deserve it. Even the most self-interested and self-promoting CO has an interest in seeing you perform well and being promoted if that performance justifies it. It is not a zero-sum game. If you hear this excuse, you are face-to-face with the reason the complaining officer was not promoted.

"I tried to get good assignments, but the detailer dealt me a bad hand." Your assignment officer deals in a market of matching people to billets and trying to make you and your prospective commanding officer happy. Most officers in the marketplace are seeking the most professionally enhancing assignments—that is, assignments that, if performed well, give the incumbent a leg up before future screening and promotion boards. Many are called and few are chosen for the plum assignments. It is a simple matter of arithmetic.

At the lieutenant and lieutenant commander level, those desired assignments are as department heads in ships, subs, or squadrons. The detailer, the placement officer (who represents your future commanding officer), and your future skipper want the best match of skills for those important and desirable jobs—and they want the best performers in them.

Detailers have a good sense of the quality of your performance record. To help them understand that record, they have a rough summary grade as to where you stand in the talent pool. Their boss is looking over their shoulder to see that the best go to the best (that is, the most demanding and therefore most desirable) jobs. Detailers who play favorites do not last very long. So, when you hear the excuse that someone was mishandled by the detailer, it means in most cases that the speaker's record simply was not strong enough to make the cut for the best jobs.

Advice for Those Who Have Missed a Hurdle

In the Navy marketplace, it is comparative performance that counts. That is why it is a good idea to review your jacket. Better yet, get a senior friend to go over your record with you and get some sense as to how you stack up. As you go over your record, fitness report after fitness report, to note how you stack up, read the numbers in the promotion recommendation section as well as the words. Did your CO indicate that you are qualified for the next step up the promotion ladder? If not, and you are still aboard, you need to get that individual to counsel you on what you need to do to get that qualification.

"My ship (or squadron) was cliquish; you were either on the boss's team or you were not." The speaker is by self-definition an outsider. There are "horizontal cliques"—that is, cliques or groups made up of peers who happen to like each other's company. It is nothing different from the social selection that goes on in all parts of any society, including the schools we attended before entering the service. Although the value of being a member of such groups is overrated, and the payoff is mostly in increased self-esteem, there is an understandable disappointment in not being included. But such exclusion rarely damages an otherwise good officer's promotion prospect.

"Vertical cliques," where they exist, can be more damaging to the command and the individual who is not a member. A vertical clique is a group that crosses major seniority boundaries. The basis for group cohesion may be social, regional, or, in rare cases, commissioning source background. Such vertical cliques are credibly viewed as a system of favoritism. Although I have seen such cliques in industry, I have not seen them in a ship's wardroom. The officer who perceives a vertical clique may instead be seeing a group of top or (more rarely) bottom performers who seek some form of kinship and ease of interaction with like-minded individuals. I have never met a CO or XO who would foster such an atmosphere. Their best interest does not exclude anyone.

"I made a single mistake, and it did me in." This is a rare admission. The statement may well be true, but the mistake may not have been a small one. And in a competition of the best, when the call may be close, one mistake may be one too many. It is a tough world, and in the Navy, it is meant to be tough because people's lives are at stake.

Usually, a mistake made as a junior officer is more easily and rapidly put aside than one made at a more senior grade, where the selection screen gets much finer. I have known flag officers who made mistakes when they were junior officers and rose to outlive them. It is more difficult to overcome similar mistakes in the grade of commander and captain, but in some cases, officers have had so much potential to offer the Navy that their career has been saved to realize that promise.

"My spouse wanted me to accept a shore assignment." Blaming your spouse or pointing to conflicting family obligations that take the speaker off the career track are prima facie evidence of a self-imposed (perhaps with the best of reasons) limit on promotability. The reasons may be valid enough, but there are enough other candidates for promotion without such problems that the Navy picks its future leadership from their number.

"I was unlucky." Luck plays some part in every career, but my experience tells me that it is seldom the decisive factor. Admiral Benitez reminds us, "There is an unexplainable sequence in life with mysteries that defy rational explanation. Don't waste time lamenting the capriciousness of the unexplainable."[3]

At the extreme, bad luck (events beyond your control to avoid or prepare for) can be decisive, but much more often, it is not. Most of what passes for good luck is meticulous preparation for the unexpected and the unknowable. You must be prepared to accept responsibility for bad luck as well as good fortune. If bad luck dogs your career and good fortune always seems to go to your competitors in the race, you need to look within to change things.

A common theme in all these explanations and complaints is that it was somebody else's fault that you failed of selection. Blame placing is not a desirable attribute of future commanders. On the other hand, there are responses that one rarely hears, which show honest introspection and opportunity for personal growth.

Rarely Heard Explanations and Complaints

"It took me a while to get my stuff together." This officer was a slow starter, and a fast finish cannot make up for some disadvantages. The race most often goes to those who both start and finish fast.

"I relied on my Naval Academy education and coasted for too long." Some Naval Academy graduates mistake a good grounding in the naval profession as sufficient to ease their promotion path to command. This is a variant of the slow-starter excuse mentioned above.

"My marriage was going bad, and I was distracted." The reader will not get any lectures here—suffice it to say a marriage that is cross-threaded with your career is a great disadvantage as you try to advance in your profession. You may have to choose between the two, and the process can be exceedingly painful, not only to your marriage but also to your future prospects in the Navy. This is something to bear in mind when you choose your spouse and when that individual chooses you: you may be deciding not just on your life partner but on your career and your success in it as well.

"I was running with a bunch of superstars." The implication is that come FITREP time, these superstars got the best reports in a very competitive environment. I would observe: welcome to your future in the Navy. As you get more senior, you are always running with superstars, officers who have screened through a very competitive selection process. In some ways, having tough competition as a junior officer is the best thing that can happen to you. First, it forces you to be on your professional toes and perform at a higher level. Second, you can learn from them. And, finally, as they (and you) progress through your careers together, you have an opportunity to foster strong friendships with the future leaders of the Navy.

"I mistook my skipper's efforts in counseling as harassment." Rarely will a CO, XO, or department head not make the effort to straighten you out and point out shortcomings in your performance. They will go further and give you a program for getting back on the right track. This is not harassment. But they are not social workers. You must sense when you are entering shoal water by asking the right questions, reviewing your record, taking your performance and received guidance seriously, and resisting the comfortable and smug feeling that you are on the right track. Above all, you must resist the notion that the world is out of step and you are not.

"I had my chance and muffed it." Your opportunities come in many forms—and sometimes they are deeply buried behind a seabag full of problems. It is often easier to push the problems aside and look for the opportunities. Opportunities have two overriding attributes: they are wrapped in hard work needed to solve problems, and they involve the risk inherent in making important decisions that can decide your career. As stated earlier, there is no golden road to good performance and advancement in your naval career. The channel is littered with the wrecks of careers ended by a lack of hard work, innate ability, or decisiveness.

"Thank you for the call—what do you suggest I do next?" This has happened, and the officer on the other end of the phone realized that the board decision cannot be undone, and the next step is to seek the counsel of others to decide what comes next.

At some point in our careers, we all fail to select for something, and at some point, our military career will be over. The question will be how you deal with the ultimate decision, and how you are willing to move on (and move up?). When I called two very good friends to notify them that they failed to select for O-6, I engaged in follow-on conversations with them and their spouses about options, opportunities, and likelihood of selection based on follow-on tours. These were very difficult conversations, as I knew the officers and their families intimately. I had assigned them to their current positions and knew the importance of roles they had played and the personal sacrifices the family made along the way. Both, who continue to be good friends, chose to retire and pursue other careers: one rose to be a presidential appointee in the Department of Veterans Affairs, and the other started a defense support company and within five years had received a Department of the Navy award as an exceptional small business. Sustained superior performance is a lifelong personal attribute.

We all know someone picked up above zone. We also know folks who were surprising "no-shows" on the promotion list. I believe the system is as fair as can be and that we each have a personal role to make sure that our records fairly reflect what our contributions have been and show that we have the experience and expertise to take the next good hard job. This is your career, as is the next position outside the Navy—make the most of it, and start with the thought that it's going to be great!

22

SOME PARTING SHOTS

> What greater satisfaction is there in life than in bringing your ship safely into a snug harbor after an arduous voyage when it seemed the elements conspired against you and you bore the responsibility for the ultimate outcome?
>
> —Anonymous retired officer

In the original edition of *Career Compass*, Rear Admiral Winnefeld closed with his "Parting Shots" of personal reflections that would leave any Navy officer to ponder how they got where they were and if they were on track to reach their deliberate career goals.

Considering the vast experience and insight of the admiral, I wish to honor his career by including his thoughts intact, and to simply lead with my own parting shots for your consideration.

If I were to sit with Ensign Rau today, what would I have to say that would encourage and enable him to be the very best naval officer that he could be?

For me, lessons in three parts are easier to explain and remember. As I reflect on my Navy career, I put my significant lessons into three bins: Join the Navy—See the World, Taking the Long View, and When in Command, Command.

Some Parting Shots

Join the Navy—See the World

That was the slogan on posters to promote service in the Navy back in the late 1960s. I grew up in a small town in New Jersey and had rarely traveled outside the state borders. I was ready to spread my wings and go to places that I had only seen in *National Geographic* magazines. In 1970 I thought the most likely destination was in the South China Sea, off the coast of Vietnam. World events changed my itinerary, but later I did make several deployments to the South Pacific and South China Sea, and instead of going to war, I made port visits to the likes of Australia, New Zealand, Taiwan, New Guinea, Vanuatu, Ulithi, and American Samoa.

From West Coast home ports, I made official and personal visits to Korea and Japan to map out the wartime service of my father-in-law in Korea and my father on the island of Okinawa. After years of challenging the Russian Navy in seas around the world, once the Soviet Union was disestablished, I was able to visit with my Russian Navy counterparts in Moscow and St. Petersburg. And a wartime engagement did come my way as part of Operation Desert Storm in 1991. Besides supporting the land effort from an aircraft carrier, we did visit ports in the Arabian Gulf, Red Sea, and Indian Ocean.

Can you be committed, persistent, and flexible enough to see where the winds might blow and how you might take advantage of the new challenges and opportunities in the Navy? With time, things change, yet my goal to serve and see the world was met as the tours and deployments took me to unknown (to me), important, exotic, and exciting places. It may not need to be repeated, but some of the assignments I received were because I had established a reputation, and past performance in hard jobs set me up to be considered for the next challenging positions. As I moved through my Navy career, this initial goal of service and adventure was always in my mind. What made it better was to enjoy some of these adventures with good shipmates and my wife.

Taking the Long View

While teaching short classes at OCS, I was disappointed by discussions with so many candidates who were focused on all they could do during their five-year contract. I had to remind them they had a minimal obligation of five years, and they were not under a contract (like the enlisted Sailors, who have an end of active obligated service). On the old officer ID cards, the expiration date was "INDEF" (indefinite)." Past your minimum obligation, you continue to serve until you or the Navy decide it is time to leave. Currently, common access cards have an administrative renewal date—which is not an end date of your obligation. You would be limiting yourself by setting the minimum time to serve and keeping that date in focus. The advice has always been: if the Navy is no longer fun and you don't feel like you are contributing or growing . . . only then should resignation or retirement be considered.

For our family, the first time we even considered resignation or retirement was at year twenty-three of service. To that time, we had "detailed ourselves," meaning we had worked with mentors and detailers and executed a career map that kept me in upwardly mobile, hard community assignments and kept our family for extended periods at duty stations where the benefits of community and schools fit well. At year twenty-three, in a good job and a great community, I received a call that I would be pulled early . . . and that I could not turn down these orders, as "you were recommended for this new (first-time) billet" (two of the warnings from chapter 17).

That is when we realized we actually could refuse the orders, but to do so, I would feel obligated to submit my retirement papers.

We did postpone a response to the detailer but said that we would be glad to report to the CNO's Strategic Studies Group (as the first engineering duty officer selected), and committed to whatever and wherever the detailer would send us in the follow-on tour.

An important part of managing our career was the positive approach to each assignment. Several of the jobs were very demanding and mentally taxing, but as we entered each new position, my wife would simply repeat (and believe), "It's going to be great!"

When I received a letter from the Bureau of Naval Personnel that I had reached the statutory retirement point for an O-6, I fired back a request for just one more year (which was promptly denied). We had taken the long view, and we were serving the Navy for the long term, which has been graciously extended as I continue to teach as a civilian at the U.S. Naval Academy.

When in Command, Command

The question arises as to how comfortable you are when decisions need to be made and others are looking to you for an answer. Of course, depending on the situation and your experience, you may not have the answer at hand—but do you know where to find it?

My first and most important leadership lesson was presented on my very first day, on my very first ship. I was assigned to be the main propulsion assistant (MPA) on the USS *Fox* (CG 33) in San Diego. While completing SWO School and the main propulsion assistant hot-plant course, I had been communicating (by letter) with the incumbent, a Lieutenant (j.g.) Burbridge. I had the specific day I was to report to the ship and a very vague understanding of his turnover expectations.

I reported to the ship the night before my report date, stayed aboard, and was up early and ready to meet Lieutenant (j.g.) Burbridge in the wardroom for breakfast. His plan was still undefined. We walked to the flight deck for quarters, and the leading chief called the divisions to attention (more than sixty Sailors representing M Division [machinery] and B Division [boilers]). Burbridge said, "At ease men, this is Ensign Rau.... He is in charge!" And he walked away! This was my very first day, on my very first ship. The chief appeared unphased and waved his open hands as if to say, "Ensign, the floor is yours!"

Hopefully, a turnover like this is not in your future, and hopefully you would be prepared just in case it does happen. The very important lesson at that moment was that no one in the formation challenged the statement that I was in charge! The chief had many more years of service, and there was one Sailor who was twice my age. Yet as the O-1, with less than one day on board, I was in charge. So—command! I obviously had a lot to learn, but the Sailors accepted me and expected me to quickly learn the people and systems in my divisions, to invest my energy to care for their welfare, and to be courageous to make some hard decisions.

By the time my extended MPA tour was over, *Fox* had an MPA, an M Division officer, a B Division officer, and two Battle Es painted on the stack. At each following duty station, I requested short, concise turnover plans, because I was eager to be in charge, and I was willing to command.

Hopefully these personal reflections will encourage you to serve with enthusiasm and pride and to seek promotion and command. The path may be hard, but the instruction is simple: demonstrate sustained superior performance. It's going to be great!

Parting Shots: A Philosophy to Live and Serve By

One's life is defined by choices (e.g., to marry or not) and imperatives over which one has no control (e.g., inherited genes). Much of the point of life is to expand one's choices to provide sufficient scope to live a useful and satisfying life. For many of us, our choices include selecting a college or university to attend, deciding on an academic major, choosing an occupation, selecting immediate or deferred payoffs, proposing marriage, deciding whether to have a child, deciding when to change jobs or retire, and so on.

Having a choice is a necessary but insufficient condition for living a useful and satisfying life. One must make good choices. But even good choices are insufficient. One must also invest the effort needed to realize the decisions made. This trilogy of strategies, that is, maximizing the scope of choice, making the right choice, and then working to realize the benefits of the path taken, applies to success in the naval profession. There are pitfalls at each decision point. Some officers limit their choices too early in their careers, others make what will be the wrong choices because of insufficient information or stubborn adherence to the preference of the moment, and still others do not apply themselves to pursuing the benefits of the correct (for them) choice. As one of the quotes at the beginning of this book said, "We may give you advice, but we cannot inspire conduct."

The two most significant obstacles to optimizing choices and to professional advancement are lack of self-knowledge and impetuosity. These hazards are particularly salient to the officer candidate and junior officer. The transient glamour or immediate financial rewards of a warfare specialty or the attractions of a particular home port can turn the novice's head when that individual should be taking the longer view. Even as a midshipman your own predilections and circumstances are conspiring to limit your future choices, choices that will affect you for a lifetime. You may be drawn to aviation or SEAL training—or the Judge Advocate General's (JAG) Corps—by glamorous portrayals on TV or in a popular film of the moment. But you may know in your heart that you do not have the hand-eye coordination, temperament, physical stamina, or penchant for diligent study to perform well in one of these or other specialties.

It became apparent to me while I was going through flight training that some of my flight training classmates were unsuited for a career in naval aviation—and that they knew it once they started the training. In some cases it should have been apparent to them before they applied. So, they started their careers with failure as a result of impetuosity or lack of self-knowledge. Some transferred to other specialties, some were killed in training accidents, and the remainder muddled through to get their wings but had unsatisfying or short careers. The point here is that deliberation, knowing yourself, and honestly confronting your capabilities and motivations are the best investment you will ever make in life and in a naval career. This self-knowledge cannot come soon enough—and in the best of circumstances should occur before you put on the uniform.

Part of this self-knowledge is to gauge your willingness to bear the costs. The reasons for a lack of success in a naval career are many. Some misunderstood the degree of personal sacrifice entailed in a successful career. Some were lazy and did not overcome the inertia of taking the easy path. Still others fooled themselves into thinking they would do all right once they got the right job or the right boss. Others entered into a wrong marriage and saw it destroy their career prospects. And a few were unlucky. But very few were unlucky for an entire career. It is not enough to want to be a captain or flag officer; you must be willing to pay the personal price that such a promotion

Some Parting Shots

entails. That price includes self-denial, hard work, taking charge of your own life, and accepting responsibility for what happens along the way.

Such advice is easily said, but hard to do. What are the warning signs of potential failure?

1. Going with the flow—letting stronger people take charge of your life
2. Leaving the hard work to others or believing that such work has no payoff; believing there is an easier way or that there are workable shortcuts for smarter people (like you)
3. Making excuses for failure rather than accepting personal responsibility; blaming others (spouse, skipper) for your shortcomings and disappointments
4. Enjoying it now rather than later
5. Failing to gauge your own potential and limitations before being forced to
6. Gradually falling into the "loser" mode—unpaid bills, marital problems, mediocre fitness reports, gaining weight—and looking for escape mechanisms such as resignation and job change, early retirement, extramarital affairs, divorce, bankruptcy, or blaming someone else.

What are the signs of potential success?

1. A fierce and uncompromising acceptance of responsibility for your own shortcomings and for discharging your obligations to others
2. A "do it now!" mindset
3. An ability to deny yourself the easy path, the slick solution, the luxury of cutting corners, getting the benefit now and paying the price later (or getting someone else to pay the price for you)

4. An ability to do what you must do but hate to do—but doing it well anyway (a good piece of advice from my Naval Academy classmate Adm. Kinnaird McKee)
5. An ability to put mission first, your people second, and yourself last
6. An ability to confront the problems of life and service honestly and unemotionally build solutions that work.

In the modern trendy world there is a new expert: the "life coach." These individuals help (for a sizable fee) the wealthy and powerful organize their lives because their clients have neither the time nor the skills to do it for themselves. They provide tools of discipline to their clients by helping them organize their free time (e.g., schedule time with family for Saturday from two to four in the afternoon), their personal finances, their personal entertaining, their fitness regimen, and their workload (real or perceived) and by arranging specialized counseling when needed. Although most of us would snicker at the apparent preciousness and pretentiousness of such a concept, the fact is that most of us must undertake these functions on our own—and sometimes we do not do them very well. For better or worse, most of us must perform the duties as our own life coach. We can learn from the life coach concept by standing back and looking as objectively as we can at how we are performing. Put on your own life coach hat occasionally and examine yourself critically but constructively. What is out of balance in your life? Where do you need to improve? Where do you need help? This self-counseling can be refreshing if it is honest and tough enough.

Where Is the Fun in the Naval Profession?

You will often hear the bromide, "If you aren't having fun, you aren't doing it right." Most of the prescriptions for self-improvement in

Some Parting Shots

this book require hard work, attention to detail, and a tenacious devotion to duty. To some this will not sound like fun. But the "fun" in the naval profession comes from the satisfaction of a job well done, making a contribution that makes a difference, and the comradeship of those who, like yourself, like challenges, like to be tested and found up to the mark, and see the humorous side of Navy life. It is fun to serve with people you respect, with whom you have suffered hardships and experienced danger, and who appreciate your contribution to the unit, the mission, the service, and the nation.

There is an analogy in athletics. Much of any sport is hard work and dedication. But most athletes pay the price, enjoy the competition, and cherish the high of winning. You do not have to be an athlete to be a good naval officer. You can get the same elation by solving problems, guiding others to achieve a common objective, and outsmarting a capable enemy. Successful naval officers, whether athletes or not, do not experience fun through self-indulgence, "good times," or ego trips. Rather, they enjoy being part of a team with an objective higher than themselves, overcoming adversity, and being part of a band of brothers and sisters who have met the test of courage, honor, and commitment.

Taking the Long View

In this book we have taken a cruise together through the Navy's assignment and promotion systems, and the time has come to say goodbye. I have left much out of the log of this journey—such as the paramount importance of personal integrity, the need for courage in the face of adversity, and the importance of preparing yourself to handle the stress of the long watches and the demands of duty when it would be easier to fall into bed and let someone else worry about things. I have emphasized the importance of performance, hard work, situational awareness, and the sensors that will keep us out of shoal water.

My seaman's eye tells me that most of the officers I served with were capable of making flag. Many wanted to return to civilian life early in their naval careers. Others were unwilling or unable to make the sacrifices that would have been required to reach the top of their profession. Many others were proud and able Sailors but fell to the numbers attrition exacted at each promotion point. The point is that if you get your commission, advancement to the top of your profession is within your reach. Whether it is in your grasp is largely up to you—not some impersonal system that devours its own and not some crap game contingent on the roll of the dice. This judgment will not be popular with some readers who see the opponent as an impersonal system programmed to frustrate them at every turn. My counsel to those who believe that comfortable judgment is that life will be difficult for you in or outside the service. The service has merely held you accountable more quickly than you like.

One of the characteristics of successful naval officers (of whatever rank) that I find most appealing and warranting of respect is their fearless acceptance of responsibility. Most do not whine, make excuses, or look for scapegoats. They realize that their profession is a hard one that requires personal commitment, courage, and integrity and that the risks to themselves and to their unit can be very high. But they are not reckless risk takers. They take risks when the stakes are high enough and the odds give them a chance to succeed. They ask nothing more. One of the intangible benefits of naval service is that people of this type surround you: they lead you, they follow you, and they give you a hand when you offer it. No man or woman can ask for more.

The naval profession is one long love affair. There are bumps and valleys, but there are also indescribable highs. There are parts of

Some Parting Shots

your career that you would just as soon forget: the chewing out that you received—and richly deserved, the near miss with another ship or a nearby shoal, the frequent reminders that you are not as good as you think you are, the gradual understanding that you depended on others more than they depended on you, and your first time in combat and the nagging question of whether you would measure up. But there are other parts you will never forget: the "well done" from a respected senior for a job completed in the face of great difficulties; the glory of homecoming after a long, arduous, and successful deployment; the sense of comradeship with your fellow Sailors and aviators; and the joy and pride on a well-deserved promotion or decoration and the attendant knowledge that you had measured up. This glow will follow you into retirement. There is no more emotional event outside of marriage that compares to a reunion with old shipmates, with the reliving of shared experience, hardship, and danger. They are living testimony that you served well and with a band of heroes. No one can take that experience away from you. Indeed, those who have not served will not even understand it. But you will, and your shipmates will. What you are experiencing is the joyful song of a grateful nation saying thank you.

—Rear Adm. J. A. Winnefeld Sr.

APPENDIX A

Dilemmas and Paradoxes in a Naval Career

Much of the material in this appendix has already been covered in a different form in this book. Still, some elaboration might be useful, focusing on specific dilemmas that are likely to be faced in a naval career. Look on this material as a group of extended footnotes placed here to avoid cluttering up the text. To some, these dilemmas are more imaginary than real. Some see life as a simple series of choices to be made rationally—a misleading caricature of the philosophy laid out in the last chapter. That extreme perspective gives short shrift to officers who do not see things in black-and-white terms and have healthy doubts about their ability to select achievable goals and the competence to navigate a safe course through hazards.

Therefore, this appendix is for officers who reflect on their situation and not for officers who are never afflicted with self-doubt. Few recommendations are offered in the discussion that follows. A good coach can assist in the problem-solving and having you articulate and structure the problem. When that is in hand, solutions often supply themselves. It helps to think about problems in advance so that we recognize them when they appear and have already done some intellectual spadework in preparing for them.

Loyalty versus Integrity

Some will assert that there is no dilemma: that a loyal officer is an officer with integrity, and vice versa. We should not conclude that too quickly, however. Although loyalty to an institution such as the Navy might partially coincide with integrity, loyalty to a person (for example, a senior or classmate) can conflict with integrity as it applies to an institution. This dilemma can occur as early as midshipman days when one is tempted or asked to cover for or "not bilge" a classmate or teammate. One of the realities of academy and college life is a fierce loyalty to contemporaries: classmates, fraternity brothers or sorority sisters, teammates, and company mates. Loyalty to persons is an integral part of daily life, and the institution, although important, is seen as "them" and not "us." The honor systems of the service academies sometimes flounder on this dilemma because the integrity ethos is so foreign to much of our upbringing and natural inclinations. Loyalty is relatively easy, and integrity is often difficult and exacts consequences. If you have not already faced this dilemma as a midshipman or officer candidate, you will at some point in your career as a naval officer.

When a choice is posed between loyalty and integrity, it means the system's integrity is breaking down. The danger in loyalty is that it is too often diverted to a person or an office rather than the institution that the person or office serves. But it is the person or office one encounters daily, not the largely faceless institution. One forms friendships and personal bonds not with institutions, but with real people. They are classmates, shipmates, imperfect bosses, and subordinates. One learns to love, respect, and cherish them (or most of them), but those feelings must end when duty is encountered. That is the hard decision facing officers who would do their duty. Seniors in particular must not impose the need for choice, either knowingly or unknowingly, on subordinates.

Still, loyalty—consistent with one's duty—to one's commanding officer and one's shipmates is what holds the institution together. The answer is to be loyal right up to the point where integrity is compromised. All the societal pressures of the naval service argue for carrying loyalty over to the domain of integrity. The best naval officers resist that pressure even at the risk of destruction of their careers and lives. The only consolation in all this is that anything worthwhile demands a high price. It is demeaning to attempt to do what is right and then whine about the price to be paid.

Family versus Service

In most cases this dilemma is slow to emerge, but with the passage of years and the presence of a growing family, it becomes more salient to the serious naval officer. Some couples see no dilemma: the service comes first, and family hardships are accepted. Such difficulties as family separations, moving to areas with substandard schools, deployments, and income that falls short of perceived needs are accepted in the name of the service. At the other extreme are couples who sacrifice everything for the welfare of their children or their own creature comforts or to get ready for an eventual return to civilian life. Most of us lie between these two poles and have to make decisions from time to time that judge the balance at that point. And the point of balance does change as the years pass.

For example, caring for a child with disabilities can lead to a fundamental decision of accepting an assignment that is less career-enhancing but is located where medical help is more readily available. A working spouse whose income is needed to meet anticipated college education expenses has his or her own career needs that are often in conflict with those of the Navy spouse. Painful decisions sometimes must be made. Some marriages are torn apart by these decisions. In some cases where both spouses are in the military, the problems that need to be solved can be even more painful. There is no one-size-fits-all advice for these circumstances.

But there are some general guidelines that can prepare for the pain of unwanted dilemmas.

Prepare
Make every effort to discuss possible career and family conflicts before the marriage. People have a general reluctance to do this. Other things are foremost at this point in a relationship. Moreover, there is an unshakable belief that love can conquer all. No amount of prior talk will head off an unwanted decision, but prior discussion will make it easier to deliberate the matter when it comes and head off recriminations that stand in the way of a good solution.

Seek Counseling
I am not talking here about marriage counseling (though some may be needed), but about counseling with friends, mentors, skippers, and parents to talk the problem through and be sure you have not overlooked some important options and factors in your decision. Your XO or CO is a good place to start. Before entering such counseling, think through each aspect of the problem: budget impact, schools, medical care, career prospects of both spouses, and so on, and lay out the costs and benefits.

Do Not Decide in Haste
Most career dilemmas simmer over an extended period, and few require fast solutions. Turning your back on a Navy career may be the best solution for you, but once the decision is made, it is nearly irrevocable.

Have a Plan
Once you decide, lay out the steps necessary to realize the decision. Indicate subsequent decision points. Adjust the plan as

circumstances change. The detailers have templates that can help to visualize the timelines for major career milestones.

Accept the Consequences of Your Decision

Once you decide, there will be temptations to have second thoughts, to try to return to the decision and tinker with it to reduce its unpleasant consequences. This is a natural tendency, and its anticipated occurrence should be part of your original decision and subsequent planning. Circumstances can change, but be careful not to be blown by the latest wind or a sense of remorse.

Formal Education versus Sea Service

This dilemma may be faced both early and late in a career. Do you go for that postgraduate course, the war college tour, or a course that more firmly keeps you in competition for the next screening or promotion hurdle? Those who are more conservative and are already preparing for the eventual return to civilian life often opt for formal education. Their calculation is that more education is useful both in service and in a post-service career. They are already hedging their bets. Or perhaps they like the career path that more professional education might lead to. For example, they are attracted to an engineering duty or aeronautical engineering duty career—transferring from the unrestricted line. Further formal education is needed in those and other specialties. So, your decision to continue your education may have two dimensions: preparing for civilian life and preparing for a service career field that requires more formal education. Most billets requiring such education are ashore.

In the past (say, until the 1970s), an officer could do both. More formal education was often a career plus. When I was a junior officer, it was expected that we, as professional officers, would attend a postgraduate course of instruction. Articles in the *Navy Times* correlated the selection opportunities of those who had attended such instruction and those who had not. The nod usually went to those who had furthered their education. The subject has become more clouded because of the extension of training pipelines for assignment to sea duty and the proliferation of short and/or off-duty soft-skill master's degree programs. The result is that today the benefits of postgraduate or war college instruction in furthering your career are more problematic. How can we structure this dilemma so as to provide some guidance for the ambitious officer? You might find the following set of questions useful. Prioritizing your answers to these questions and being brutally honest with yourself will tell you a great deal about your true motivation.

1. Do you really enjoy going to sea, or do you consider it simply a necessary step in your career progression?
2. Which do you enjoy more: leading Sailors, or managing resources? Also, what do you like better: tactical decision-making afloat, or advising top leadership on major decisions?
3. Is command at sea or attainment of high rank your ultimate career objective? (Be reminded that the in-residence postgraduate degree is now required prior to assuming major command.)
4. What is your *principal* motive for pursuing a postgraduate course of instruction? To be a better sea officer? To be a better officer in shore billets? To get ready for a civilian career? To add to your résumé? For the intellectual challenge? To prepare for a possible transfer to the restricted line or staff corps?
5. Which do you enjoy more: arguing from the abstract to the specific, or from experience to general rules?

6. Which do you enjoy more: challenges to your intellect, or challenges to your character? You must choose even if your first answer might be both.
7. Is qualifying for a rewarding second career of major concern to you?

Although these questions are simplistic and limit choice, your honest answers will tell you much about yourself and the directions you might take. Bear in mind that the Navy needs postgraduate-educated officers for a large number of billets (mostly ashore). Note, though, that here we are discussing what you want to do, not what the Navy needs to staff the shore establishment. In deciding on postgraduate instruction, you need to integrate the following: staying well positioned for successful sea command (if that is what you want), picking a career path that is most attuned to your skills and interests, and building an experience and intellectual base for your second career.

Short Career versus Long Career

Some would turn this dilemma into an actuarial and future income discounting problem. They would argue that if you consider both your first and second career income streams (including your Navy retired pay), you are better off financially by retiring when you are first eligible to do so. Many in this group also argue that you are better off taking an early rather than a later Social Security benefit. This simple formulation—particularly persuasive to career enlisted personnel—overlooks that intangible called workplace satisfaction and the largely unknowable chances of achieving higher rank.

If one were to proceed narrowly on this basis, one would aim at promotion to the rank of commander and retire at the twenty-year point before coming up before the captain promotion board. On the way, you would pick up as much education at Navy expense as you could and, after selection to commander, seek jobs that enhance your civilian résumé. Your last sea duty might be as a lieutenant commander on the verge of selection to commander. This approach will appeal to some. But for others, a twenty-year commitment to a job whose only satisfaction is the prospect of early retirement would argue that you should leave even sooner—perhaps at the first release from active duty date or after your additional obligated service for postgraduate education date.

I would offer an alternative strategy, one foreshadowed in the early chapters of this book. I suggest entering the service with an initial commitment to the long career strategy. In your early twenties, you cannot be very sure of where and how you want to spend the rest of your life. Throw your hat in the long career ring, work hard and perform well, and see how it goes. Keep your options open as long as you can. Get in the habit of doing a good job because you are committed to a long career and because it is the most valuable tool you will have—long career or short career. If things do not go well for you or you become disenchanted with the prospect of further service, you can shift gears. At the ten-year point in your career, you should have a pretty good idea of how the prospect of a long career suits you.

Comparative versus Absolute Performance

This is a dilemma of delusion—often self-delusion. You will encounter officers who throughout their careers have been advised by their bosses, mentors, and friends that they are doing an excellent job and should get over the next hurdle easily. Many of these officers will not be screened or selected for promotion not because they were not good enough but because others were better qualified or showed more promise for future development in the eyes of selection boards. Like it or not, life and a naval career are competitive. You are expected to be good—and the vast majority of officers are—but the prize goes to the best. One may argue that the best are not always selected, but from the very beginning the objective of selection and promotion systems is to select the best. By definition, "best" is a comparative term.

It is easy to persuade yourself that you are doing a good job and should be promoted or screened. But look around you. In looking at your fitness reports, ask yourself: Am I the best in my unit? Am I really putting out my best effort? Could it be that I am deluding myself? Am I ranked among the highest in the comparative evaluation that is part of every fitness report? The words may be nice, but the breakout is the key. Are you a "packer," or do you break out? If you do not know, your detailer can tell you.

Earlier in this book, I pointed out that if you are the best, the best assignments will seek you out. If you constantly have to push the system, argue with your detailer, or campaign for a good job, you should be receiving a message. At a minimum, you are not yet among the best. This is not to say that you should not take an active role in managing your career, but if you always seem to find "the system" pushing against you, you are seeing the first harbingers of career trouble.

Wait a minute, you may say. The picture you are painting is a dog-eat-dog career environment, a zero-sum game, a winner-take-all race, and I am not interested. Most career officers do not agree with such a sour appraisal. Good comparative performance is vital to screening and promotion, but your focus should be on pushing yourself, not on how your shipmate-competitors are doing. You should be focusing on doing your job well, not taking on the role of the referee at the finish line. Over a full career, I have observed some very strong wardrooms and ready rooms, ones that were loaded up with superb officers. Yes, their skippers had to rank them, but most of those top-running officers did not let that fact poison their relations with each other. Most became close friends, and over time all or almost all were screened and promoted.

Some pose the dilemma: should I be a good shipmate or a strong competitor? The answer is easy: both. The strong competitor part should focus on one's own performance, not on how the others in the race are doing. There is a payoff in this attitude that goes beyond eventual screening and promotion. You will be a good shipmate, you will enjoy your tour, and, if in the end you are denied the trophy, you will know that you gave it your best and can take pride in a race well run.

APPENDIX B

The Junior Officer's Professional Library

Midshipmen have regularly asked me for a reading list, and my regular answer is, "The best books to read are on my nightstand right now!" The list continues to change and includes the classics, Navy-centric titles, military history, fiction, do-it-yourself guides, and other texts written by my associates at the Naval Academy. You might be concerned about the thought of a personal library. You might be thinking, "When do I have time to read all that stuff, and why do I want to lug that stuff around with me?" (Your tablet is an easy storage device!) Every mentor will tell you that you should (no, must!) continue to pursue self-improvement—to expand your understanding and knowledge. Reading (to include podcasts and audiobooks) is the doorway to your moral and mental development. A good professional library is one of the pillars of your professional growth.

This start of a booklist will serve you well throughout your naval career (and will be updated over time). You will see that the Naval Institute Press is a ready source for most of them. The institute is the principal publisher of naval professional books worldwide.

When asked by your subordinates, be ready to recommend some books for their professional development and personal enjoyment!

About Your Duties

McComas, Lesa A., and J. D. Kristensen. *The Naval Officer's Guide*, 13th ed. Annapolis, MD: Naval Institute Press, 2019.

O'Neil, Samantha. *The Newly Commissioned Naval Officer's Guide.* Annapolis, MD: Naval Institute Press, 2025.

Stavridis, James, and Robert Girrier. *The Division Officer's Guide,* 12th ed. Annapolis, MD: Naval Institute Press, 2004.

———, Robert Girrier, and Fred Kacher. *Command at Sea,* 7th ed. Annapolis, MD: Naval Institute Press, 2022.

———, Robert Girrier, Tom Ogden, and Jeff Heames. *The Watch Officer's Guide,* 16th ed. Annapolis, MD: Naval Institute Press, 2020.

About Your Professional Skills

Barber, James A. *Naval Shiphandler's Guide.* Annapolis, MD: Naval Institute Press, 2020.

Crane, C. E., and Robert Shenk. *Guide to Naval Writing,* 4th ed. Annapolis, MD: Naval Institute Press, 2024.

Llana, Christopher B., and George P. Wisneskey. *Handbook of Nautical Rules of the Road: A Convenient Take-Along Guide for Sail and Power Boaters.* Annapolis, MD: Naval Institute Press, 1991.

Montor, Karel. *Naval Leadership: Voices of Experience,* 2nd ed. Annapolis, MD: Naval Institute Press, 1998.

Schratz, Paul. *Submarine Commander: A Story of World War II and Korea.* Lexington: University Press of Kentucky, 1988.

Stavridis, James. *Destroyer Captain: Lessons of a First Command.* Annapolis, MD: Naval Institute Press, 2008.

———. *The Sailor's Bookshelf: Fifty Books to Know the Sea.* Annapolis, MD: Naval Institute Press, 2021.

Strunk, William, Jr., and E. B. White. *The Elements of Style,* 4th ed. New York: Allyn and Bacon, 2000.

Symonds, Craig. *Nimitz at War: Command Leadership from Pearl Harbor to Tokyo Bay.* New York: Oxford University Press, 2022.

Toll, Ian W. *The Pacific War Trilogy.* New York: W. W. Norton and Company, 2012.

Wray, Robert, Andrew Ledford, John Mustin, and Theodore LeClair. *Saltwater Leadership: A Primer on Leadership for the Sea Services*, 2nd ed. Annapolis, MD: Naval Institute Press, 2021.

Zumwalt, Elmo R. *On Watch.* Arlington, VA: Zumwalt and Company, Inc., 1976.

About the Service

Benitez, Rafael. *Anchors: Ethical and Practical Maxims.* Annapolis, MD: Annapolis Publishing Company, 1996.

Burgess, Richard R. *The Naval Aviation Guide*, 5th ed. Annapolis, MD: Naval Institute Press, 1996.

Calvert, James. *The Naval Profession*, rev. ed. New York: McGraw-Hill, 1965.

Conetsco, Cherlynn, and Anna Hart. *Service Etiquette*, 5th ed. Annapolis, MD: Naval Institute Press, 2013.

Cutler, Thomas J., Mark Hacala, and Paul Kingsbury. *The Bluejacket's Manual*, 26th ed. Annapolis, MD: Naval Institute Press, 2023.

Filbert, Brent G., John Baker, and Mark Jameson. *Naval Law: Justice and Procedures in the Sea Services*, 4th ed. Annapolis, MD: Naval Institute Press, 2023.

Mack, William P., and Royal W. Connell. *Naval Ceremonies, Customs, and Traditions*, 6th ed. Annapolis, MD: Naval Institute Press, 2004.

Noel, John V., Jr., and Edward L. Beach. *Naval Terms Dictionary*, 5th ed. Annapolis, MD: Naval Institute Press, 1988.

Stavridis, Laura Hall. *The Navy Spouse's Guide*, 2nd ed. Annapolis, MD: Naval Institute Press, 2002.

About Your Character Development

Sileo, Tom, and Tom Manion. *Brothers Forever: The Enduring Bond Between a Marine and a Navy SEAL that Transcended Their Ultimate Sacrifice.* New York: Da Capo Press, 2014.

Skerker, Michael, David Whetham, and Don Carrick. *Military Virtues: Practical Guidance for Service Personnel at Every Career Stage.* Howgate, UK: Howgate Publishing, 2019.

Stavridis, James. *Sailing True North: Ten Admirals and the Voyage of Character.* London: Penguin Books, 2019.

Stockdale, James. *Thoughts of a Philosophical Fighter Pilot.* Stanford, CA: Hoover Institute Press, 1995.

———, and Sybil Stockdale. *In Love and War, Revised and Updated: The Story of a Family's Ordeal and Sacrifice During the Vietnam Years.* Annapolis, MD: Naval Institute Press, 1990.

Washington, George. *George Washington's Rules of Civility & Decent Behavior in Company and Conversation.* New York: BN Publishing, 2007.

NOTES

Preface
1. President Dwight D. Eisenhower at the National Defense Executive Reserve Conference, November 14, 1957.
2. Bible, New International Version, Matthew 24:6.

Chapter 1. Performance
1. Oath of office required by Section 3331, Title 5, U.S. Code. Officers traditionally recite the oath upon promotion, but as long as the officer's service is continuous, this is not required. "I, do solemnly swear (or affirm) that I will support and defend the Constitution of the United States against all enemies, foreign and domestic; that I will bear true faith and allegiance to the same; that I take this obligation freely, without any mental reservation or purpose of evasion; and that I will well and faithfully discharge the duties of the office on which I am about to enter. So help me God."
2. OPNAVINST 3120.32: "Standard Organization and Regulations of the U.S. Navy." "Action: a. All members of the U.S. Navy will comply with the regulations prescribed in this instruction.
b. Commanders, commanding officers, and officers in charge will give the contents of this instruction the widest possible dissemination to ensure that each Sailor in the U.S. Navy is aware of their responsibility for complying with the regulatory portions."
3. Col. Arthur Athens, USMCR (Ret.), director of the Vice Adm. James Stockdale Center at the U.S. Naval Academy, recites the 3 Cs as principles required for any junior officer to lead well: competency, compassion, courage.
4. BUPERSINST 1610.10E, "Navy Performance Evaluation System."

5. Skipper—A term of endearment in the Navy (and sports). The word "skipper" originated from the Dutch word *schipper*, which means "a person who commands a ship." In my career and in this text, skipper is interchangeable with commanding officer.
6. According to the PERS-4 Mission Statement, the detailing triad strives to meet the needs of the Navy, career needs, and personal preferences in a most responsive, courteous, and service-oriented manner.
7. Personal conversation with a mentor and former boss.

Chapter 2. Your Boss Wants to See You Promoted but Needs Your Help

1. NAVADMIN 056/24, "Retention Excellence Award," is the CNO's direction for the annual award given to commands that meet their specific reenlistment rates and remain below the Navy's attrition benchmark.
2. A total of twelve Navy commanding officers were fired in the first six months of 2024. The Navy relieved sixteen commanding officers in 2023. The reasons presented fall into the category of "loss of confidence in [their] ability to lead." https://www.navytimes.com/breaking-news/2024/06/07/navy-fires-uss-somerset-commanding-officer/.
3. Report on the fire aboard USS *Bonhomme Richard* revealed that the "initial response to the July 2020 fire that destroyed the multi-billion-dollar amphibious assault ship *Bonhomme Richard* was uncoordinated and hampered by confusion." Megan Eckstein, "New Details Emerge About the 2020 *Bonhomme Richard* Fire, Ahead of Censure of Three-Star," *Defense News*, July 5, 2022, https://www.defensenews.com/naval/2022/07/05/new-details-emerge-about-the-2020-bonhomme-richard-fire-ahead-of-censure-of-three-star/.
4. "Eleven Gen. George Patton Quotes that Show His Strategic Awesomeness," Military.com, August 5, 2021, https://www.military.com/history/2021/08/05/11-general-george-patton-quotes-show-his-strategic-awesomeness.html.
5. Private conversation with previous commanding officer of the Blue Angels.

6. Tania Lombrozo, "This Could Have Been Shorter," NPR, February 3, 2014, https://www.npr.org/sections/13.7/2014/02/03/270680304/this-could-have-been-shorter.
7. Adm. J. M. Richardson, "The Charge of Command," April 2018, https://www.mynavyhr.navy.mil/Portals/55/Career/Detailing/Officer/Documents/Charge_of_Command.pdf?ver=N3AgFh9i8dYoS6F1azqDXw%3D%3D.
8. USNA and Naval Service Training Command, *Officer Professional Core Competencies Manual*, April 2019.
9. George Washington, "The Rules of Civility," https://www.mountvernon.org/george-washington/rules-of-civility/.
10. Conversation with a previous boss who has been my lifetime "champion!"

Chapter 3. What Are They Saying About You?

1. John Masters, *Bugles and a Tiger: A Personal Adventure* (New York: Viking, 1956). This book is an excellent distillation of experience gained the hard way in adjusting to service life as a junior officer.
2. When I retired and was in the job search process, I had a four-hour interview, or more of a presentation, with one company. At the end they asked, "Do you have any questions?"
I responded, "I have been here for almost four hours and you have asked me no questions (other than the one just asked). . . . What do you want to know about me?" Their response: "We know all about you and know you would be a great fit for our company. Our intention is to give you all that you need to know about us so you can decide if it is the right fit for you." Your reputation precedes you most anywhere!
3. Sue Russoniello, University of Pennsylvania career services, https://ulife.vpul.upenn.edu/careerservices/blog/2010/06/14.

Chapter 4. What Should They NOT Be Saying About You?

1. Rafael C. Benitez, *Anchors: Ethical and Practical Maxims* (Annapolis, MD: Annapolis Publishing, 1996).

Chapter 5. Leveling the Playing Field

1. MyNavy Coaching pilot: All Sailors are invited to participate in voluntary one-on-one professional coaching. This service is being offered as part of a study being conducted by the Talent Management Center of Excellence; https://www.mynavyhr.navy.mil/Career-Management/Talent-Management/Coaching/.
2. "Speed Mentoring" events are voluntary events where midshipmen can be quickly introduced to staff officers who are in a career field the midshipmen are considering. Voluntary on behalf of both parties, the partnership lasts as long or as briefly as it is helpful for the midshipmen to be ready for commissioning and off to their initial duty station.
3. You may ask for an example of how the mentor's advisory function works in practice. Within the engineering duty community, all O-5 selects are assigned an active duty senior officer as their mentor. The assignments are made according to the intended future assignments (program management, shipyard maintenance, and so forth). The arrangement obviously is not as informal as previously stated, and the routine of engagement and depths and topics for discussion were unspecified and determined by the pair. The outcomes of the relationships varied significantly. Based on the strength of the relationship, the time, and interest, some pairings lasted a tour, and others a lifetime. I was one of the fortunate mentees who, once assigned a senior mentor, continued regular communication to discuss career, family, and then retirement highlights and low points. The partnership was helpful support for my follow-on Navy tours, and our family friendship has continued for more than thirty years. A pinnacle of this relationship was when I was the invited speaker at my mentor's retirement (as a Navy rear admiral), and he was the invited speaker at mine.
4. Harvard University's Executive Leadership Coaching mastery session costs $2,990 for the two-day certificate program. https://professional.dce.harvard.edu/programs/executive-leadership-coaching-mastery-session/#outcomes.

Notes to Pages 47–57

5. The GROW model of coaching questions is the foundation of MyNavy Coaching: https://www.mynavyhr.navy.mil/Portals/55/Career/Talent Mgmt/Coaching/GROW%20Model%20Handout_FINAL.pdf?ver =OTbE-K8K2libh1uOmW1Teg%3d%3d.
6. There are stories of Adm. Elmo Zumwalt (CNO in the 1970s) and Navy Secretary John Lehman (1980s) using their position to bring former colleagues and friends into influential positions—arguably, in order to facilitate change.
7. Preliminary Navy manning report, prepared by USNA Office of Institutional Research, January 26, 2024.

Chapter 6. Spring Training

1. Robert D. Heinl, *Dictionary of Military and Naval Quotations* (Annapolis, MD: Naval Institute Press, 1966), 88.
2. "The Board of Inspection and Survey (INSURV) was initially established by Congress in 1870, with legislation enacted in 1882, to inspect our Navy ships and to report on their readiness. It is a thorough inspection that examines ships against Navy standards to determine readiness in myriad areas. The inspection is designed to be taken 'in stride' and as an 'open-book test' (the standards available beforehand)." See https://www.insurv.usff.navy.mil/.
3. Edward Arthur Burroughs, *The Fight for the Future* (1916). Such is a description of life in the Navy according to a British navy lieutenant.
4. "Job Role: Physical Training Instructor," https://www.royalnavy.mod.uk/careers/roles/physical-training-specialisation-direct-entry.
5. Navy Physical Readiness Program Guide 4 (body composition assessment): https://www.mynavyhr.navy.mil/Portals/55/Support/Culture%20Resilience/Physical/Guide_4-Body_Composition_Assessment_BCA_JAN_2023.pdf?ver=V-3wCu5X586wXMTCa4C2ag%3D%3D.
6. Navy Physical Readiness Program Guide 5 (physical readiness test): https://www.mynavyhr.navy.mil/Portals/55/Support/Culture%20Resilience/Physical/Guide_5-Physical_Readiness_Test_PRT_JAN_2023.pdf?ver=OlmOLoZTfCA641JUkAnIaw%3D%3D.

Chapter 7. Do You Shine in the Career Marketplace?
1. C. S. Forester, *Hornblower and the Hotspur* (Boston: Little, Brown, 1962), 13.
2. T. B. Buell, *Master of Seapower—Biography of Fleet Admiral Ernest King* (Annapolis, MD: Naval Institute Press, 2012).

Chapter 8. Been to School Lately?
1. NAVADMIN 263/18: Update to Navy Graduate Education Program.
2. USNA Strategic Plan 2020, "Qualifications of a Naval Officer," https://www.usna.edu/StrategicPlan/_files/docs/USNA-Strategic-Plan.pdf. Quotes from letters of John Paul Jones compiled by Augustus C. Buell: "It is by no means enough that an officer of the Navy should be a capable mariner. He must be that, of course, but also a great deal more. He should be as well a gentleman of liberal education, refined manners, punctilious courtesy, and the nicest sense of honor."
3. OPNAVINST 1520.23C, "CNO Instruction Concerning Graduate Education," https://www.secnav.navy.mil/doni/Directives/01000%20Military%20Personnel%20Support/01-500%20Military%20Training%20and%20Education%20Services/1520.23C%20w%20CH-3.pdf.
4. MyNavy HR links to the different community sites with instructions and templates for graduate education applications: The talent management board is used to ensure that the best and most fully qualified officers are assigned to billets or special programs that reward performance. The board is conducted semiannually in September and March.
5. Chairman of the Joint Chiefs of Staff Instruction, "Officer Professional Military Education Policy," May 15, 2020, https://www.jcs.mil/Portals/36/Documents/Library/Instructions/CJCSI%201800.01G.pdf.
6. Jim Stockdale, *Thoughts of a Philosophical Fighter Pilot* (Stanford, CA: Hoover Institution, 1995).
7. The American Association of Colleges and Universities defines liberal education as an approach to undergraduate education that promotes integration of learning across the curriculum and cocurriculum,

and between academic and experiential learning, in order to develop specific learning outcomes that are essential for work, citizenship, and life. https://www.aacu.org/trending-topics/what-is-liberal-education.

Chapter 9. Sea/Shore Rotation and Homesteading
1. Private conversation with PERS-41 staff.
2. Private communication with a CO on a Rota-based ship.
3. The Enhanced Defense Cooperation Agreement allows for cooperative training and operations between the U.S. and Philippine militaries. The impact for the Navy is access to previously used air fields and port access for Navy ships.

Chapter 10. Command and Staff Assignments
1. Communication with current PER-41 detailer and review of surface warfare officer community brief.
2. CNO outlines the Force Design 2045 plan in the Navigation Plan of 2022 (which includes unmanned vessels—a new twist in command opportunities!).
3. James Stavridis and Robert Girrier, *Command at Sea*, 6th ed. (Annapolis, MD: Naval Institute Press, 2010).
4. U.S. Navy Regulations 1990, chapter 8.
5. James Stavridis, *Destroyer Captain: Lessons of a First Command* (Annapolis, MD: Naval Institute Press, 2008).
6. Rear Adm. George Yount, USN (ret.), has been guiding me with career and life advice for more than thirty-five years.

Chapter 11. Washington Duty
1. F. W. Kacher and D. A. Robb, *Naval Officer's Guide to the Pentagon* (Annapolis, MD: Naval Institute Press, 2019).
2. MyNavy HR OPNAV site directory, https://www.mynavyhr.navy.mil/References/Site-Directories/OPNAV/.
3. Kacher and Robb, 83.

Chapter 12. Career Tracks for the Unrestricted Line

1. MyNavy HR, public site for Navy flag officer roster: https://www.mynavyhr.navy.mil/Career-Management/Detailing/Officer/Flag/Flag-Management/.

Chapter 13. Promotion to Flag Rank

1. The eighteenth-century French author Voltaire is credited with first coining the phrase "with great power comes great responsibility." However, it became popularized in American folklore through Stan Lee's Marvel Comics character Spider-Man. Former CNO and Chairman of the Joint Chiefs of Staff Adm. Michael Mullen, USN (ret.), and Rear Adm. George Yount, USN (ret.), have provided edits to the original text of this chapter by Rear Admiral Winnefeld.
2. Reference for the flag officer promotion selection board precept is DoD Instruction 1320.14, "DOD Commissioned Officer Promotion Program Procedures," December 2020.
3. List of all Navy flag officers is available at the Flag Matters website: https://www.mynavyhr.navy.mil/Career-Management/Detailing/Officer/Flag/Flag-Management/.

Chapter 14. Awards and Decorations

1. SECNAV M-1650.1, *Navy and Marine Corps Awards Manual* (August 2019).
2. Personal conversations with U.S. Naval Academy senior officers who have served in recent combat.
3. The "C" device is awarded to service members who demonstrate meritorious acts and achievements performing while under combat conditions. The "R" device is for individuals who have displayed meritorious acts using a weapon system or other warfighting activities that directly impacted combat operations.
4. Private communication between recent board member and author.

Chapter 15. Pass the (Social) Polish, Please

1. *George Washington's Rules of Civility and Decent Behavior in Company and Conversation.* Copied out by hand as a young man aspiring to the status of gentleman, George Washington's 110 rules were based on a set of rules composed by French Jesuits in 1595.
2. C. Conetsco and A. Hart, *Service Etiquette*, 5th ed. (Annapolis, MD: Naval Institute Press, 2009).
3. Navy Social Media Handbook, 2019, https://www.csp.navy.mil/Portals/2/documents/downloads/navy-social-media-handbook-2019.pdf.

Chapter 16. The Navy Spouse and Family

1. Current officer scenarios include an increase in dual-military couples or spouses with significant career positions that impact career paths. Additionally, new rules for maternity and paternity leave highlight the Navy's acceptance of major business rules and the importance of supporting the family through significant inflection points of their lives and career.
2. Laura H. Stavridis, *Navy Spouse's Guide*, 2nd ed. (Annapolis, MD: Naval Institute Press, 2002); J. D. Collins, Lauren Tamm, and "Jo, My Gosh," *Modern Military Spouses: The Ultimate Military Life Guide for Spouses and Significant Others* (self-published, 2016).
3. Jim Stockdale and Sybil Stockdale, *In Love and War* (Annapolis, MD: Naval Institute Press, 1990).
4. Jennifer Barnhill, "Why Divorce Is Particularly Hard on Military Families," Military.com, June 22, 2023, https://www.military.com/daily-news/opinions/2023/06/22/why-divorce-particularly-hard-military-families.html.
5. Barnhill.

Chapter 17. Assignment and Placement Officers

1. Home page and primary reference for Bureau of Naval Personnel: https://www.mynavyhr.navy.mil/Navy-Personnel-Command/.

2. Private conversations with community manager in N41 (SWO).
3. Secretary of the Navy order for convening fiscal year 2025 promotion selection boards September 7, 2023.
4. Looping is Navy slang for a position where you are authorized to wear the shoulder aiguillette. The number of braids is equivalent to the admiral's stars.

Chapter 18. The Fitness Report System

1. BUPERS Instruction 1610.10F, *Navy Performance Evaluation System*, December 1, 2021, Change 1, August 18, 2022.
2. Handout from and discussion with PERS-42 community manager.
3. BUPERS Online; https://www.bol.navy.mil/bam (CAC required).

Chapter 19. Screening and Promotion Boards

1. Private discussions with recent O-6 selection board members.
2. MyNavy HR for unrestricted line officers, https://www.mynavyhr.navy.mil/Career-Management/Community-Management/Officer/Active-OCM/Unrestricted-Line/.
3. Secretary of the Navy letter, "FY-25 Active-Duty and Reserve Navy Flag Officer Promotion Selection Board Precept," September 7, 2023.

Chapter 20. Advice for Midshipmen

1. There is one additional practical leadership point for midshipmen. Your current military role revolves around peer leadership. Despite the four-year age or midshipman rank differential, midshipmen leading midshipmen is all about peers. The big change comes when the junior officer stands in front of a division of E-1 through E-9 Sailors, and everyone knows the O-1, with one year of experience, is in charge. As a midshipman, be thinking of your new and different leadership role once commissioned. Review and compare the oath of office for an officer and an enlisted member. You currently have a role in the "real Navy," and it is up to you to make the best of this opportunity

to hone your leadership skills. See https://www.navy.mil/About/Our-Heritage/.

2. Quote attributed to John Paul Jones:

It is by no means enough that an officer of the Navy should be a capable mariner. He must be that, of course, but also a great deal more. He should be as well a gentleman of liberal education, refined manners, punctilious courtesy, and the nicest sense of personal honor.

He should be the soul of tact, patience, justice, firmness, kindness, and charity. No meritorious act of a subordinate should escape his attention or be left to pass without its reward, even if the reward is only a word of approval. Conversely, he should not be blind to a single fault in any subordinate, though at the same time, he should be quick and unfailing to distinguish error from malice, thoughtlessness from incompetency, and well-meant shortcomings from heedless or stupid blunder.

In one word, every commander should keep constantly before him the great truth, that to be well obeyed, he must be perfectly esteemed.

Chapter 21. Advice for Those Who Have Missed a Hurdle

1. Hamilton Basso, *The View from Pompey's Head* (New York: Doubleday, 1954), 204.
2. Rafael C. Benitez, *Anchors: Ethical and Practical Maxims* (Annapolis, MD: Annapolis Publishing, 1996), 24.
3. Benitez, 16.

INDEX

admirals, 59, 86, 108. *See also* flag rank
advancement, 3, 54, 60, 96, 125, 189, 194, 201; enlisted, 52
aide tours, 137, 148–49
ambition, 6
appearance, 30, 56, 127
assignments, 1–5; command and staff, 81–87 (*see also* detailers) dilemmas, 153–55; family constraints, 136; graduate school, 68, 72–73. *See also* Washington duty
assignment officers. *See* detailers
attitude, positive/negative, 28–31, 53, 87, 218
aviator, 29, 31, 91, 99, 207; command screen, 100; production tours, 147; qualifications, 180; shore duty, 68, 71, 76, 103
awards, 118–23, 176. *See also* decorations

Barry (USN destroyer), 86
Benitez, Rafael, 28, 156, 188, 192
Bennis, Warren, 22
Blue Angels, 103
Board of Inspection and Survey (INSURV), 53
boiler technician, 63
Bonaparte, Napoleon, 81, 118
briefer/briefings, 15–16; at boards, 171
Bureau of Naval Personnel (BUPERS), 139, 154, 199; BUPERS Online (BOL), 169
Burke, Arleigh, 59, 177

cadets (OCS), 28, 179. *See also* midshipmen
California casual dress, 126
can-do, 12
Captain's mast, 20
career advice, 6, 12, 76, 149; failed promotion, 184–95 (*see also* mentors/mentoring); for midshipmen, 177–83; at Pentagon, 96–97
career tracks, 98–107. *See also* detailers; education; mentors/mentoring

Central Command, U.S., 101
Chief Petty Officer (chief) 29; MCPON, 73
choices, 201–2; career, 71, 182; FITREPs, 159–61
character, 18, 23, 28, 215; leader of, 2, 40, 113
chain of command, 93
characteristics, desired and valued, 17, 24, 33, 59–60, 206; flag, 112; spouses, 134–35
chief engineer, 24, 50
Chief of Naval Operations (CNO) 2, 95, 132, 147; instructions, 2; Strategic Studies Group, 196
Chief of Naval Personnel (N1), 95
cliques, 34, 43–44, 191
coaching, 37–42, 50, 155. *See also* mentors/mentoring
Cold War, 119
Cole, Harley, 83
combat operations, 101, 203
command, 8, 81–87; chain of command, 17, 31, 34, 43 (*see also* commanding officer); post command, 7, 104, 150
commanding officer (CO, commanders), 10, 21, 49, 72, 81–82, 85; in command 34, 83–87, 188–89; for FITREPS, 4–5, 11–12, 100, 136, 142, 157–68; as mentor, 40, 42, 49, 72; PME for, 69

communication, 17, 20; with detailer, 69, 78; skill, 42, 51
competence (professional), 17–18, 53, 91, 113, 182
competition, 37, 95, 100, 110, 173
Constitution, U.S., 21
contemporaries, 23, 25–26, 45, 58–62, 151, 163
Cornwallis, William, 60
correspondence courses, 70, 72, 180
counseling, 42, 157, 168, 188, 194, 204, 212; mid-term, 5, 165; performance, 159–62
counter culture, 44
COVID-19, 93
credentials, 7–8, 63, 150, 176; joint, 77
cross-deck, 5
cross-rate, 5
Crowder, Doug, 96

damage control, 13
decision making, 34, 48, 61, 187
Decatur, Stephen, 10, 21
decorations, 8, 118–23, 176. *See also* awards
Defense Enrollment Eligibility Reporting System (DEERS), 133
Defense Officer Personnel Management Act, 116
department head, 12, 21, 99, 146, 163, 180–82; awards, 120;

Index

billets, 146, 172; fleet up, 49–50; schools, 67
Department of Defense, policy, 70; flag positions, 111–13
deployment, 75, 78; combat, 54, 101; family separation, 136; FITREPs, 163; overseas, 5, 92, 133
descreening, 176
detailers, 42, 63–65, 107, 169; detailer's triad, 6, 97; mechanics of detailing, 7–9, 140–47, 152–55, 172, 184, 190; as mentors, 82, 198–99; misconceptions, 151–52, 190; priorities, 67–71, 78–80, 94–95, 137; timelines, 213
dilemmas, 209–18
disappointment, 77, 86; career, 181; in FITREPs, 169; in personnel system, 151–52; in promotion, 185–87, 191
division officer, 29
Don't Ask, Don't Tell (2010), 132
Dunn, Robert, 1, 58
Duty Preference Card, 70, 142

education, 7, 180; postgraduate, 63, 65–74, 146; professional military, 69–70, 103–4; verses sea duty, 213–14
email, 33
Emerson, Ralph Waldo, 36

evaluations. *See* fitness report
Eversail (fictitious Navy ship), 24
excuses, 11, 53, 169, 203, 206
executive assistant, 115, 149
executive officer (XO), 5, 21, 163, 165
experience, 7, 35, 63, 82, 87 (*see also* mentors/mentoring); operational, 145
expertise, 18, 53, 73; in-rate, 103; for promotion, 109, 111, 144, 148

failure, 31; potential, 203, to screen, 154, 169, 188–90. *See also* disappointment
family/family life, 22, 27, 92; expectations, 65, 69, 71, 78; message from CNO, 132–138; moves, 78–79; separations, 75; Washington duty, 95–96
Fighter Weapons School (Top Gun), 16
fitness report (FITREP), 4, 156–70; competitive, 105, 122, 154, 167–68; desirable and undesirable content of, 162–65; use by detailers, 42, 145, 151; format and timing, 158–59; marketability, 62–63; not observed, 146; for performance, 3, 12, 21; relook after passed over, 189–91; at selection boards, 91, 136; what

fitness report (FITREP) (*continued*)
    is said, and not said, 159–65;
    your input, 5, 166–67, 170
flag lieutenant / aide, 148–49
flag rank, 59, 115, 205; awards, 120;
    characteristics required 63, 70,
    100–1, 112–14; executive
    assistant, 105; flag matters, 106,
    139; joint billets, 103, 147;
    promotion boards, 108–12,
    172–73; Washington tours,
    89–91; youth vs. age, 116–17
Flatley Jr., James, 59
fleeting up, 14, 48–49, 85
fleet replacement squadrons, 68, 147
Forester, C.S., 60
forward deployed, 4, 79
Fox (USN cruiser), 24
Franklin, Benjamin, 27
fun, 21, 56, 89, 95, 181, 205; no
    longer, 198

gapped, billets, 7, 78, 144, 150
geographic bachelor, 78
GI Bill, 72
Gilday, Michael, 132
gloomy Gusses, 13
Golden Anchor Award, 10
gossips, 33
graduate education. *See* education
GROW (goal, reality, options,
    will), 41. *See also* coaching
Gulf War, 101

hail and farewell, 95
Halsey, William (Bull), 61
Harris, Clay, 139
homesteading, 75–79, 116
Hornblower, Horatio, 60
Howard, Michelle, 59

individual augmentation (IA), 101
integrity, 61, 205–6; of boards, 176;
    versus loyalty, 209–11
Iraq, 119

joint assignments, 63, 66, 69–70,
    90, 103–5, 147
joint chiefs, 59; staff tours, 105
Joint Forces Staff College, 77
Jones, John Paul, 66
judge advocate general (JAG), 17
junior officer, 12; career tracks,
    98–107; fleeting up, 48–49;
    reputation, 23–27; Washington
    duty, 11, 96

Kacher, Fred, 89
King, Ernest, 50, 61

leadership, 85, 111; challenges,
    47–51, 82; in command, 10, 129;
    development, 8, 70, 72, 86, 103,
    147, 179; evaluation of, 3, 21, 28;
    flag, 111; teams, 13, 42
left seat–right seat, 48
life-of-the-party officers, 34–35, 164
loners, 35, 113

Index

looping, 149
loyalty, 35; ADM King, 61; for enlisted, 182; for a group, 43–44; verses integrity, 209–11
luck, 4, 8, 59, 109, 182; part of career, 192–93, 202

machinist mate, 63
Marine, 13
marketplace, 58–64
Martin, Steve, 9
Masters, John, 23
Masters in Business Administration (MBA), 71
medals. *See* awards/decorations
mentors/mentoring, 25, 38–43, 69, 86, 136; detailing, 78, 104; for midshipmen, 182
midshipmen, 1, 28; advice for, 177–83; connections, 44–45; leadership, 87; mentoring, 39, 128. *See also* Naval Academy
midterm counseling, 5
moaners, 31
Moorer, Thomas, 59
Mullen, Michael, 59
murder boards, 16
MyNavy Coaching, 38

Naval Academy, 1, 66, 74, 127–28; advice for MIDN, 177–83; alumni, 95; mentoring, 39–40 (*see also* midshipmen); ship selection, 79

Naval Institute, U.S., 73, 83–84, 126
Naval Leadership and Ethics Center (NLEC), 85
Naval Postgraduate School (NPS), 66, 102. *See also* postgraduate education
Naval Reserve Officer Training Corps (NROTC), 56
Naval War College, 66–68, 73
Navy administrative message (NAVADMIN), 174
Navy and Marine Corps Awards Manual, 120
Navy Performance Evaluation System, 3, 156–70. *See also* fitness report (FITREP)
Navy Personnel Command, 139, 154, 172; billets, 50, 88, 105; boards, 172; detailing, 50, 62, 147 FITREPs, 159, 169–70
Navy regulations, 85
Navy's Social Media Handbook, 129
needs of the Navy, 6–7, 63, 78, 97, 110, 138
networking, 92
Neversail, (fictitious Navy ship), 22
Nimitz, Chester, 59, 61, 81

oath of office, 2
obligation, 35–36; family, 186, 192; in FITREPs, 162; mentoring, 42; minimal service, 198; to Oath of Office 2, 9

Officer Candidate School (OCS), 23
Officer Personnel System. *See* detailers/detailing
Officer Professional Core Competencies, 19
opportunism, 32
orders, 153; assignment/PCS, 49, 68, 73, 75, 80, 133, 137, 142; discussions with detailers, 146, 154, 185; giving, 11
overseas tours, 5, 75, 79–80, 103–5, 137, 149

passed over, 184–195
Pasteur, Louis, 47
Patton, George, 15
performance, 1–9; and assignments, 81, 104, 141, 153; comparative and absolute, 101, 105, 216–17; descriptives, 28–30 (*see also* fitness report); flag rank, 109–10, 113; forecast of future, 46, 107; mentoring, 38–42
Pentagon, 68, 73, 88–97; flag matters, 106, 109. *See also* Washington duty
Permanent Change of Station (PCS), 75
physical fitness/readiness, 54–55
pipeline, 2, 68–70; for command, 85, 100; selection, 182; training, 66–67, 117, 143, 180, 214

placement officers, 139–44, 150–51. *See also* detailers/detailing
planning board for training (PB4T), 56
postgraduate education, 63, 67–70, 116, 146, 216
Post, Emily, 124
precommissioning, 5
preference sheet, 142, 151
production pipeline, 147
professional military education (PME), 66, 69–70, 103–104
promotion, 1–3, 8–12, 189–192; above zone, 185; attitudes towards, 11–12; attributes for, 58–63, 216; boards, 8, 21, 151, 161–62, 171–76; education for, 68–70; failure for, 189–193 (*see also* flag rank); recommendations for, 158–61, 168
protégé. *See* mentors/mentoring
public speaking, 15–16, 51

qualifications, 7; for promotion 142, 166, 172; pipeline, 2, 19, 142, 150, 180; warfare, 67–68, 76, 99

ready room, 13, 15, 29, 30–36, 44, 129, 151
red hots, 13
refresher training, 49

Index

regulations, 31–32, 85, 124, 179; changes, 129
reputation, 22, 36, 181; ADM King, 61; detractors, 28–34; jobs, 4; personal, 12, 20, 136–38; professional 15–16, 23–27, 39, 45, 48, 62, 67, 82, 113, 173–78
restricted-line, 5, 67, 81, 91, 179, 214
retention, 10, 24, 44, 50, 72, 116
Retention Excellence Award, 10
retirement/retired, 116, 120, 133; as mentors, 23–25, 149; your decision, 26, 110, 138, 154, 173, 185, 198
Richardson, John, 18
ripped out, 7, 147
risk taking, 4, 59–60, 206; career, 173, 185, 194, 211; in orders, 67, 69, 77, 154

Sailor, 19–24; at mast, 20; awards, 120–22; duties, 13; experience, 14, 53, 106; fitness, 55; leadership, 99, 111; spouses, 132; standards, 129
Schildt, Goran, 98
screening/selection boards, 91, 94, 101, 121, 160, 163, 168, 172–76
sea daddy, 39, 142
sea duty, 66–70, 75–76, 101; focus on, 82

Secretary of the Navy, 110, 114–16, 171
selection boards: and fitness reports, 4, 21, 101, 110–16, 136, 159–62, 174–75, 217
service assignment, 39–40, 182
service jacket, 26, 62, 123, 133
ship, shipmate, self, 6
shiphandler, 29, 111
shipyard duty, 102
ship over, 10
shore duty/tour, 5–6, 63, 67–69, 82, 102–6, 143, 186; detailer's input, 140–48; flag tours, 106; rotations, 75–79, 98–100; Washington, 88, 93
situational awareness (SA), 31, 48, 113, 169, 180, 206
skipper. *See* commanding officer
social media, 30–33, 128–29
social polish, 124–31, 148
Spider-Man, 109
spouses, 22, 77; in detailing, 152, 192–95, 211–12; and family, 132–38
Spruance, Raymond, 59, 61
Standard Organization and Regulations, 2
staff duty, 82, 86–87
Stavridis, James, 59, 85, 88
Stockdale, James, 72; Sybil, 134
Stolen Valor Act, 122
Subic Bay, 79

submarine officers, 2, 71, 91, 99–100, 133
subspecialty, 63, 153
surface warfare officers (SWO), 77, 79, 99–100, 142
Systems Command, 88, 104–5

talent management board, 69–70
test pilot school, 68, 103
throwaway tour, 71
training pipeline, 66–67, 180, 214

undergraduate education, 66, 73. *See also* education
unrestricted line (URL), 81, 91, 140, 213; career tracks, 98–107

Veterans Affairs, Department of (VA), 195
Vietnam, 119, 188, 197

war college, 22, 66–73, 104, 116, 153, 213–14
wardroom, 13, 15, 26, 33–36, 44, 49, 67, 77, 125–29, 151, 162, 191, 200; lizard, 29
warfare pins/specialties, 8, 59, 82, 91
warfighter/warfighting, 5, 36, 54, 65, 67, 179
wartime preparation, 53–54
Washington duty, 87–97, 116. *See also* Pentagon
Washington, George, 20, 124, 130
watch standers, 29
water walkers, 58
Winnefeld Sr., James, 90, 130, 134, 156, 179, 196, 207
work-life balance, 6, 66, 138

Zumwalt, Elmo, 59

ABOUT THE AUTHOR

Douglas H. Rau graduated from the U.S. Naval Academy (USNA) in 1974 and served thirty years as a surface warfare–qualified engineering duty officer (EDO). His sea tours included chief engineer of USS *Rathburne* (FF 1057) and USS *Nimitz* (CVN 68). Shore tours included department head at Puget Sound Naval Shipyard, Fellow on the CNO's Strategic Studies Group, senior detailer and community manager for the EDO community, dean of engineering at USNA, and commanding officer of the Naval Research Laboratory in Washington, D.C. He is the chair and Distinguished Professor of Leadership Education at USNA. A resident of Annapolis, Maryland, his additional interests include being an enthusiastic supporter and ring/rink/court announcer for Navy club sports.

The Naval Institute Press is the book-publishing arm of the U.S. Naval Institute, a private, nonprofit, membership society for sea service professionals and others who share an interest in naval and maritime affairs. Established in 1873 at the U.S. Naval Academy in Annapolis, Maryland, where its offices remain today, the Naval Institute has members worldwide.

Members of the Naval Institute support the education programs of the society and receive the influential monthly magazine *Proceedings* or the colorful bimonthly magazine *Naval History* and discounts on fine nautical prints and on ship and aircraft photos. They also have access to the transcripts of the Institute's Oral History Program and get discounted admission to any of the Institute-sponsored seminars offered around the country.

The Naval Institute's book-publishing program, begun in 1898 with basic guides to naval practices, has broadened its scope to include books of more general interest. Now the Naval Institute Press publishes about seventy titles each year, ranging from how-to books on boating and navigation to battle histories, biographies, ship and aircraft guides, and novels. Institute members receive significant discounts on the Press' more than eight hundred books in print.

Full-time students are eligible for special half-price membership rates. Life memberships are also available.

For more information about Naval Institute Press books that are currently available, visit www.usni.org/press/books. To learn about joining the U.S. Naval Institute, please write to:

Member Services
U.S. Naval Institute
291 Wood Road
Annapolis, MD 21402-5034
Telephone: (800) 233-8764
Fax: (410) 571-1703
Web address: www.usni.org

www.ingramcontent.com/pod-product-compliance
Lightning Source LLC
Jackson TN
JSHW021926011125
93490JS00001B/1